In memory of
Joan Kerns Ostling
Nyack College Faculty 1993 - 199

T. S. ELIOT:
Aesthetics
And History

821.912
E14
F87

T. S. ELIOT:
Aesthetics
And History

By Lewis Freed

Department of English
PURDUE UNIVERSITY

OPEN COURT • **ESTABLISHED 1887** • **LA SALLE, ILLINOIS**

Library of Congress Catalog Card Number: 61-11289

T. S. ELIOT: AESTHETICS AND HISTORY

©1962 by the Open Court Publishing Company

Printed in the United States of America

All rights in this book are reserved.

No part of this book may be used or reproduced in any manner whatsoever without written permission except in the case of brief quotations embodied in articles and reviews. For information address The Open Court Publishing Co., 1307 Seventh Street., La Salle, Illinois.

TO MY WIFE

TO MY WIFE

PREFACE

THIS BOOK IS CONCERNED primarily with T. S. Eliot's criticism, that is, with his theory of the nature and use of poetry; it is also concerned with certain issues raised by his criticism, issues indicated by the sub-title of the book.

The principal matter is given in Chapter VIII. The chapters preceding this serve, I trust, to place Chapter VIII in an intelligible perspective. Chapter IX offers a brief argument, supplementing, as it were, the argument implicit in the chapter on Kant.

Literary study sometimes requires an excursion into philosophy. The best that a literary student untrained in philosophy can offer is a literary treatment of such matters; for a philosophic treatment one must go to

VII

philosophers. In dealing with Kant and Bradley, I have tried to say only so much as I thought was necessary to elucidate Mr. Eliot's poetics. My experience is that, for literary purposes, if philosophic ideas cannot be made clear in a short exposition, no amount of elaboration will help. I might also say that there does not seem to be any natural beginning for the exposition of a philosopher. One starting point is as good as another, for no exposition can be clear at the start; exposition becomes clear, if it ever does, only in its development. I found James C. Meredith's Introductory Essays to Kant's *Critique of Judgement* helpful. For the treatment of Bradley I must take full responsibility.

Occasionally in the text and notes I have included parallel passages from Mr. Eliot and Bradley; but, since an entire book might be prepared of such passages, I have tried to state Bradley's position in such a way that readers familiar with Mr. Eliot's work might supply their own parallels.

Though this work does not deal with Mr. Eliot's poetry, it bears a relation to it. For myself, this study has raised certain questions about the poetry; no doubt they will also occur to the reader. But I have put off dealing with the implications for the poetry.

I wish to thank Professor Brand Blanshard, of Yale University, for bringing this work to the attention of Dr. Eugene Freeman, the editor of the Open Court Publishing Company.

May, 1962

Place yourself . . . at the centre of a man's philosophic vision and you understand at once all the different things it makes him write or say. But keep outside, use your post-mortem method, try to build the philosophy up out of the single phrases, taking first one and then another and seeking to make them fit, and of course you fail. You crawl over the thing like a myopic ant over a building, tumbling into every microscopic crack or fissure, finding nothing but inconsistencies, and never suspecting that a centre exists.

William James

ACKNOWLEDGMENTS

I WISH TO EXPRESS my thanks to the following publishers
for their kind permission to reprint material from
their works. From the following works by T. S. Eliot:
Selected Essays, copyright, 1932, 1936, 1950, by Harcourt, Brace and World, Inc., reprinted with their
permission; *Notes towards the Definition of Culture,*
copyright, 1949, by T. S. Eliot, reprinted by permission of Harcourt, Brace and World, Inc.; *Four Quartets,* copyright, 1943, by T. S. Eliot, reprinted by
permission of Harcourt, Brace and World, Inc.; *On
Poetry and Poets,* copyright, 1943, 1945, 1951, 1954,
1956, 1957, by T. S. Eliot, reprinted by permission
of Farrar, Straus and Cudahy, Inc.; *The Use of Poetry
and the Use of Criticism,* Faber and Faber, Ltd.; *The
Sacred Wood,* Methuen and Co., Ltd. From the following works by F. H. Bradley: *Appearance and Re-*

ality, The Clarendon Press, Oxford; *Ethical Studies,* The Clarendon Press; *Essays on Truth and Reality,* The Clarendon Press; *The Principles of Logic,* Oxford University Press, London. From *Philosophies of Beauty,* edited by E. F. Carritt, The Clarendon Press. From *Kant's Critique of Aesthetic Judgement,* translated by J. C. Meredith, The Clarendon Press. From the following works by A. N. Whitehead: *Adventures of Ideas,* The Macmillan Company; *Process and Reality,* The Macmillan Company. From *The World's Body,* by J. C. Ransom, Charles Scribner's Sons. From the following works by Etienne Gilson: *The Unity of Philosophical Experience,* Charles Scribner's Sons; *The Spirit of Mediaeval Philosophy,* translated by A. H. C. Downes, Charles Scribner's Sons. From *A History of Aesthetic,* by Bernard Bosanquet, George Allen and Unwin, Ltd. From *Critique of Judgment,* by Immanuel Kant, translated by J. H. Bernard, Hafner Publishing Company, The Hafner Library of Classics. From *Philosophy and Civilization in the Middle Ages,* by Maurice De Wulf, Dover Publications, Inc. From *A Companion to Shakespeare Studies,* edited by H. Granville-Barker and G. B. Harrison, Cambridge University Press. From *The Philosophy of the Enlightenment,* by Ernst Cassirer, copyright, 1951, by Princeton University Press. From *A History of Literary Criticism in the Renaissance,* by J. E. Spingarn, Columbia University Press. From *The Principles of Psychology,* by William James, Holt, Rinehart and Winston, Inc. From *The Greek Genius and Its Influence,* edited by Lane Cooper, Yale University Press.

Contents

T. S. ELIOT:
Aesthetics
And History

CHAPTER 1
THE PERFECT CRITIC

T. S. ELIOT LATELY HAS RETURNED to a theme which has been a major preoccupation of his for more than a generation. In "The Frontiers of Criticism"[1] he refers to an article he wrote thirty-three years earlier entitled "The Function of Criticism." The intervening years having brought changes in critical doctrine and practice, Mr. Eliot feels that it is time for a restatement of his position. In the earlier essay, the object of his attack, he says, was impressionistic criticism. In the later one, it is the criticism of explanation by origins, biographical and psychological, and the kind of criticism fostered by I. A. Richards. This last —"the lemon-squeezer school"—has its classroom uses, as offering exercises for pupils; but, like the first, it has its limitations and dangers. Neither type, Mr. Eliot thinks, fulfils the proper function of criticism. This function, as Mr. Eliot states it in the earlier essay, is "the elucidation of works of art and the correction of taste"; in the later essay, he changes the phrase to "promote the understanding and enjoyment of literature."

Though the tone of the two essays is different, as are the critical doctrines attacked, the thesis is the same. It is, indeed, the thesis which runs throughout Eliot's critical work. The essays and reviews which make up *The Sacred Wood* represent a consciously articulated program of critical activity. Eliot says of this volume that it is "logically as well as chronologically the beginning." It is concerned with the problem of "the integrity of poetry," and it leads to a consideration of the larger problem of "the relation of poetry to the spiritual and social life of its time and of other times." And this difference between the earlier and later criticism represents "not so much a change or reversal of opinions, as an expansion or development of interests." Moreover, we are admonished to take the distinction between these two types of problems with caution.[2]

The essay which stands first in *The Sacred Wood*, "The Perfect Critic," is perhaps Eliot's most explicit statement of his view of criticism and the relation of criticism to creation. Two other essays in the same volume, "The Possibility of a Poetic Drama" and "Dante," are important pieces in the development of his literary theory. They deal with the question of literary form and the relation of poetry to philosophy. The essay on Dante in *Selected Essays*,[3] though it incorporates the substance of the earlier and shorter essay, does not supersede it in every respect. Similarly, "A Dialogue on Dramatic Poetry," also in *Selected Essays*, presents a further stage in Eliot's reflections on poetic drama, the subject here being the relation of poetry not to philosophy, but to religion. Again, "The Function of Criticism" is in the main a restatement of positions expounded in "The Perfect Critic." Finally, *The Use of Poetry and the Use of Criticism*,[4] his most extended discussion of criticism in relation to poetry, is in one respect like his essays in practical criticism: the light it sheds on his theory is indirect, refracted from the observations on the critics he there treats of. The work offers, among other things, hints on the doctrine of "Unity," Wordsworth's "new version of Imitation," and the "auditory imagination."

Still, "Tradition and the Individual Talent" (1917) and "The Function of Criticism" (1923), which, in effect, serve as a theoretical preface to *Selected Essays*, may be taken as stating, in essence, Eliot's main critical positions. These two essays, as Eliot tells us, are related: they are concerned in general with "the problem of order," the one in poetry and the other in criticism; and the essay on criticism is "an application of the principles" formulated in the essay on the poet and tradition. As for his other important critical writings, they are consistent in purpose and method with the positions given in these last two essays, and are in effect elaborations of those positions. And this is true of his criticism of prose as well as of verse: for instance, "Andrew Marvell" (1921) and "Lancelot Andrewes" (1926) are virtually companion pieces, both being direct applications of the principles adumbrated in "Tradition and the Individual Talent."

The characteristic note of Eliot's criticism is its seriousness. Moreover, it is the gravity of his theory—his view of the nature and use of poetry—that lends weight to the technical part of his criticism. The technical critic,[5] for Eliot, is a critic only in the narrow sense; and the reason is that he does not carry his analysis of poetry to the point of illuminating life. To be sure, poetry as art has its own proper seriousness, a seriousness great enough to require the poet to sacrifice his personal interests in its behalf.[6] But poetry is something more than technical achievement, mere verbal form; it has a content, and it is thereby related to the rest of life. Though that relation, as Eliot understands it, is indirect, it is his insistence on this connection—his belief that poetry matters—that has given his criticism its general importance.

His criticism, he has told us, was undertaken in preparation for the métier of poetry;[7] it is, as he now calls it, "workshop criticism,"[8] the prolongation of the thinking that went into his writing of verse. And this is in accordance with the view expressed in "The Perfect Critic," and elsewhere, that "the poetic critic is criticizing poetry in order to create poetry." Further, in his view, the preparation for and the practice of modern poetry requires hard thinking about many things besides poetry. Such intellectual labor is necessary because the age lacks common beliefs and values, and nothing can be taken for granted. The philosophic interest, clearly, is present from the start; the spiritual

interest, though later than the intellectual one, is yet
earlier than is commonly supposed; and the social
interest is perhaps intrinsic to the others. His criticism,
then, is not only a part of his poetic activity, but both
are related to his extra-literary interests and purposes.
"A man's theory of the place of poetry," he says, "is
not independent of his view of life in general."[9]

Another mark of his criticism is the mystification it
frequently gives rise to. Consider, for example, his
dicta on poetry and personality. Poetry, he asserts,
though originating in the depths of the poet, is an expression not of personality, but of feelings and emotions
which are extra-personal. Yet he attributes the superiority of Yeats's later poetry to his earlier to the greater expression in it of a unique personality, and explains the
apparent contradiction by distinguishing the impersonality of craftsmanship and that of the poet who
turns his personal experience into an expression of
general truths.[10] Further, discussing Milton's influence
on the English language, he says it is implicitly the
whole personality of Milton which is in question—
"not specifically his beliefs, or his language or versifi-
cation, but the beliefs as realized in that particular
personality, and his poetry as the expression of it."[11]
Finally, in *The Use of Poetry*, he declares that genuine taste is "inextricable from the development of
personality and character"; and in a footnote he adds
that he refuses to be drawn into any discussion of the
definition of these two terms.[12]

Since Eliot has written between four and five hun-
dred pieces of criticism, and he has a distaste, he informs us, for rereading his prose, it is not surprising
that he is sometimes inconsistent. Of course, observa-

tions made from different points of view are not necessarily inconsistencies. Still, Eliot's criticism does seem to bring together notions which do not form a logical whole. And so far as this is the case, his criticism is logically defective. On the other hand, there is, up to a point, a logic of feeling as well as of concepts; and theories of poetry may be tested by their effect on sensibility and imagination.

In any event, the mystification is not, in general, owing to inconsistencies. The notion of personality occupies a central place in Eliot's theory of poetry, and the theory is not independent of metaphysics. The distinctions Eliot employs in discussing personality are marked by metaphysics, but metaphysics, as it were, presented without its technical vocabulary. Commentators have sometimes complained of the inexactness of Eliot's terms, though imprecision of thought and feeling is not a mark of his writing. The difficulty may be partly that, though the terms are familiar, the distinctions they express are unfamiliar. Thus he discusses poetry in terms of feelings and emotions, but he is concerned primarily not with psychology, but with objective content; his point of view is not psychological, but metaphysical. Indeed, he speaks of psychology as a "half-formed science," and he consistently deprecates the modern tendency to confuse psychology with ethics and philosophy.[13]

It is difficult to be clear about distinctions which depend on a metaphysical tradition without invoking the suppositions of that tradition. And Eliot stops short of metaphysics,[14] because that is one of the frontiers of literary criticism—though he believes that literary criticism should be completed by criticism from an ethical and religious point of view.[15]

Another source of mystification is the mixture of negation and disclaimer with positive assertion that is commonly left unclarified. Thus, for instance, in *The Use of Poetry,* after assailing the poetic theories of Coleridge, Arnold, Richards, and others, he says he has no general theory of his own.[16] It is true that he has not written a systematic treatise on poetry; that a considerable part of his criticism is practical; and that many of his generalizations occur in the context of such criticism. It is nonetheless clear that his criticism rests upon certain assumptions and is directed by certain purposes, and that it embodies a rather definite view of the nature and use of poetry.

In *The Use of Poetry,* he says: "The extreme of theorising about the nature of poetry, the essence of poetry if there is any, belongs to the study of aesthetics and is no concern of the poet or of a critic with my limited qualifications."[17] On the other hand, in "Shakespeare and the Stoicism of Seneca," he censures critics of Shakespeare for their ignorance of general aesthetics. The "extreme" of theorizing, it would appear, refers to aesthetics as a philosophic study; and the literary critic, in Eliot's view, is something less than a philosopher, though presumably he has some acquaintance with aesthetic theory. Eliot is following the common practice of differentiating aesthetics as a branch of philosophy from literary criticism as well as from the history of literature.[18]

The literary critic, one gathers from Eliot, begins

with his experience of poetry and develops his knowledge from that point.[19] He must be true to his experience, must not falsify or go beyond it. His procedure is inductive, not deductive. This, however, is but a formal distinction, a difference in point of view. Induction which is not guided by general notions is mere impressionism—the critic, for instance, must have, first of all, some working notion of poetry. Criticism, being an intellectual activity, involves judgments and generalizations. But its judgments are something less than philosophic; for their basis is not intellectual, but sensuous or emotional—the data of criticism are not concepts, but impressions or feelings. Further, the critic does not employ his impressions as a foundation on which to raise a theoretical structure; his object is not to obtain concepts to be entertained in abstraction from his experience of poetry, but to return to the poetry with improved perception and intensified enjoyment. With the critic, generalization is the ordering and forming of his impressions into a structure, and "criticism is the statement in language of this structure."[20]

The answers to the questions Eliot raises in "The Perfect Critic"—"how far criticism is 'feeling' and how far 'thought', and what sort of thought is permitted"—are, in short, that criticism is primarily "a development of sensibility," and that the kind of thought involved is the analysis and construction of "experienced sensation and feeling."[21]

CHAPTER 2

ARISTOTLE AND OTHER CRITICS

ELIOT'S PRINCIPAL CONCERN HAS been with poetic critics. Criticism with him is in the first place a preparation for and a concomitant of poetic creation. That,
at least, is the notion of criticism with which he start-
ed. He says:

> At one time I was inclined to take the extreme position
> that the *only* critics worth reading were the critics who
> practised, and practised well, the art of which they wrote.
> But I had to stretch this frame to make some important
> inclusions; and I have since been in search of a formula
> which should cover everything I wished to include, even
> if it included more than I wanted. And the most import-
> ant qualification which I have been able to find, which
> accounts for the peculiar importance of the criticism of

practitioners, is that a critic must have a very highly developed sense of fact. This is by no means a trifling or frequent gift. And it is not one which easily wins popular commendations. The sense of fact is something very slow to develop, and its complete development means perhaps the very pinnacle of civilization. For there are so many spheres of fact to be mastered, and our outermost sphere of fact, of knowledge, of control, will be ringed with narcotic fancies in the sphere beyond.[22]

One of Eliot's "important inclusions" is, as he might say, a master of fact—Aristotle. Speaking of the *Poetics*, Eliot says that "in his short and broken treatise he provides an eternal example—not of laws, or even of method, for there is no method except to be very intelligent, but of intelligence itself swiftly operating the analysis of sensation to the point of principle and definition."[23]

Aristotle, says Eliot, was a man of "universal" intelligence: he could apply his mind to diverse classes of objects, and in each sphere "he looked solely and steadfastly at his object."[24] Though this is what is called the "scientific" mind, it is, Eliot observes, exhibited by scientists only in respect to a special class of objects. The scientist, when he interests himself in literature, is likely to behave much as the ordinary sentimental person does: he finds in literature a stimulus to the indulgence of feelings which are suppressed in his special activity, the result being that he confuses the poetry with the accidental feelings which the poetry excites in him. It is better, then, Eliot says, to speak not of the "scientific," but of the "intelligent," mind. Furthermore, there is but one kind of intelligence, whether it be that of scientist, philosopher, artist, or man of letters. It is the intelligence which is disinterested or free —free of emotion irrelevant to its object, and concerned purely with satisfying the desire to know.

This ideal of inquiry, of the impersonal exercise of intelligence, presupposes the existence of objects, sensuous and intellectual, which are independent of the mind and which when perceived directly affect the sensibility. This, says Eliot, is the assumption of mathematicians, such as Pascal and Bertrand Russell, and it is the assumption also of traditional philosophy up to the time of Hegel. Eliot refers the reader to the opening phrases of the *Posterior Analytics*, where Aristotle writes, "All instruction given or received by way of argument proceeds from pre-existent knowledge." Aristotle's point is that one must assume the existence of the objects with which a discipline deals as well as the meaning of the terms employed in the inquiry.

Though Eliot makes no explicit reference to it, there is Aristotle's distinction between the practical and the contemplative intellect. The exercise of the contemplative or scientific intellect is free of the emotions arising from the operation of desire or appetite in conjunction with the practical intellect. These emotions are irrelevant to theoretical inquiry, which seeks to satisfy purely the desire to know. Further, with Aristotle, production and action are distinct aspects of the practical intellect. So, too, what Aristotle calls "intelligence" differs from prudence. "Intelligence" is merely critical, that is, operative in making distinctions, whereas prudence is imperative in the sphere of action. "Intelligence," again, works on objects of sense, and its mode of apprehension is not logical, but perceptive and intuitive. "Intelligence," as perceptive and intuitive, is analogous to—involved in, an aspect of—intuitive reason. And intuitive reason, Aristotle says, is "at once beginning and end." It operates, as it were, below demonstration, and, at the same time, it is the foundation and constant concern of demonstration. Its essential concern, it may be said, is with facts of various orders—it is the organ of vision.[25]

In Eliot's view, these several assumptions, or something like them, are essential to any responsible and intelligible theory of the criticism of poetry. "Not only all knowledge," he says, "but all feeling, is in perception."[26] If critical discourse is to have an object, there must be something, whatever it is, which we call poetry; and that something must be distinct from random personal feelings excited by the poetry. A literary critic, Eliot asserts, "should have no emotions except those immediately provoked by a work of art—and these (as I have already hinted) are, when valid, perhaps not to be called emotions at all."[27] He means, I think, that the critic is concerned with facts of a poetic order. The immediate experience, pure feeling, ought to originate as well as terminate in perception of fact. The critic analyzes and reconstructs his impressions of fact, so that his activity ends in the knowledge of something other than his subjective response. This, I take it, is what Eliot means when he says that "a critic must have a very highly developed sense of fact." It is this that sets criticism proper apart from the effusions of sentimentalism.

To the member of the Browning Study Circle, the discussion of poets about poetry may seem arid, technical, and
limited. It is merely that the practitioners have clarified
and reduced to a state of fact all the feelings that the
member can only enjoy in the most nebulous form; the dry
technique implies, for those who have mastered it, all
that the member thrills to; only that has been been made
into something precise, tractable, under control.[28]

Limited it may be, but it is not, after all, arid. In a
passage which begins with a statement about the *Divine Comedy,* Eliot says:

> The end of the enjoyment of poetry is a pure contem-
> plation from which all the accidents of personal emotion
> are removed; thus we aim to see the object as it really is
> and find a meaning for the words of Arnold. And with-
> out a labour which is largely a labour of the intelligence,
> we are unable to attain that stage of vision *amor intellect-
> ualis Dei.*[29]

That is the sense in which Eliot is a classicist in literature. And this position explains his strictures on two
forms of subjectivism—or Romanticism: in "The Perfect Critic," he denominates the one "impressionism"
and the other "verbalism" or "the abstract style in criticism." These are species of what is now called the
"emotive" use of language, though Eliot's semantics
is not, like that of I. A. Richards or Charles Morris,
based on behavoristic psychology and the philosophy
of positivism.

In one version of subjectivism, Eliot says, the critic
deals with his emotions as though they were objects
which had occasioned these emotions. Here emotion

takes the place of perception and analysis, and language grows indefinite. In the other version, the critic does indeed begin with impressions aroused by a work of art; but, in translating these, he introduces whatever personal associations the work may have revived in him. Hence what he offers is something new, though it is neither criticism nor creation, but a kind of mixture of the two.

This last is impressionism. Nor, according to Eliot, is it confined to what used to be known as "aesthetic" criticism. It is found, for example, in lectures intended to make literary works easy for beginners. The lecturer retells the story of a play or novel; gives his impressions of character, action, and motive; and supplies comment and opinion on what he considers to be the relevance of all this to life. In effect, he relives his experience of the work, and imposes that experience on his auditors. This, too, is the character, on another level, of the greater part of what is called the critical "interpretation" of a work or an author. Here again the critic commonly substitutes something of his own creation for the work of art or for the artistic spirit of the author. Both these species of impressionism are quite alien to the exercise of the free intelligence, which is "wholly devoted to inquiry."

In "The Perfect Critic," Eliot says:

Aristotle is a person who has suffered from the adherence of persons who must be regarded less as his disciples than as his sectaries. One must be firmly distrustful of accepting Aristotle in a canonical spirit; this is to lose the whole living force of him.[30]

Eliot would count the bulk of Renaissance and Neo-classic critics as sectaries rather than disciples; and in the nineteenth century he would count writers who show little or no conscious debt to Aristotle as in some respect more deeply Aristotelian than many who profess to follow him. Thus, though the Renaissance writers pay lip-service to the Aristotelian "imitation," they do not penetrate very deeply into the notion of *mimesis*. Nor, with all their talk of the "unities," do they do much to clarify the problem of dramatic form. Sir Philip Sidney, for instance, is right in principle in insisting on the observance of the "unities," but his treatise reflects not so much a deep study of Aristotle as reading in Italian criticism and Latin authors. This is also true of Ben Jonson, a more mature critic than Sidney. Jonson, it is true, understood the spirit in which Aristotle and other ancients should be examined—they are, he says, "guides, not commanders"—but he cannot be said to have advanced the Aristotelian tradition of criticism. Nor can this be said of Dryden, who, though he alters and revises, reconstructs out of old material. Dryden, moreover, tends to legislate rather than inquire, so that he is not altogether a "free intelligence." As for Samuel Johnson, Eliot finds in him, within limits, insights which at least implicitly point to a deepening of poetic form.[31]

Eliot observes that it was Horace rather than Aristotle who served as the model of criticism until the nineteenth century. Critics like Horace and Boileau deal in "unfinished analysis": their precepts appear as rules because they are empirical; they do not appear in their "most general form." Aristotle, on the other hand, carries his analysis to the point of principles which are universal and hence necessary. Here there is no legislation based on local practice and transient taste, but free assent. Thus, speaking of dramatic form, Eliot says:

> But my point is simply that the unities differ radically from human legislation in that they are laws of nature, and a law of nature, even when it is a law of human nature, is quite another thing from a human law. The kind of literary law in which Aristotle was interested was not law that he laid down, but law that he discovered. The laws (*not* rules) of unity of place and time remain valid in that every play which observes them *in so far as its material allows* is in that respect and degree superior to plays which observe them less. I believe that in every play in which they are not observed we only put up with their violation because we feel that something is gained which we could not have if the law *were* observed. This is not to establish another law. There *is* no other law possible. It is merely to recognize that in poetry as in life our business is to make the best of a bad job. Furthermore, we must observe that the Unities àre not three separate laws. They are three aspects of one law: we may violate the law of Unity of Place more flagrantly if we preserve the law of Unity of Time, or vice versa; we may violate both if we observe more closely the law of Unity of Sentiment.[32]

Eliot is aware that "Unity of Place" is not an Aristotelian doctrine; and he is also aware that Aristotle merely observes, without commendation or censure, that the tragic poets of his own day try to confine the action within certain limits of time. As for Aristotle's "unity of action," Eliot says, "And what I have denominated Unity of Sentiment is only a slightly larger term than Unity of Action." He quotes from Butcher:

> Unity, says Butcher, in his edition of the *Poetics*, is manifested mainly in two ways:
> "First, in the causal connexion that binds together the several parts of a play—the thoughts, the emotions, the decisions of the will, the external events being inextricably interwoven. Secondly, in the fact that the whole series of events, with all the moral forces that are brought into collision, are directed to a single end. The action as it advances converges on a definite point. The thread of purpose running through it becomes more marked. All minor effects are subordinated to the sense of an ever-growing unity. The end is linked to the beginning with inevitable certainty, and in the end we discern the meaning of the whole."[33]

With Eliot, then, "unity of feeling" is the essential principle of poetic form. It is the principle in virtue of which the maturing Elizabethan drama creates a single pattern out of comic and serious elements. It is exhibited, he says, in *Coriolanus* and *Volpone*. Again, in *Henry IV* the comic relief in Part I becomes in Part II "serious contrast," and "political satire issues from it." "In *Henry V* the two elements are still more fused; so that we have not merely a chronicle of kings and queens, but a universal comedy in which all the actors take part in one event." This "higher unity of feeling" is still more evident in *Twelfth Night* and *A Midsummer Night's Dream*, and it is found in *Macbeth* and

Antony and Cleopatra. Further, in estimating the success of such plays as *Measure for Measure, Troilus and Cressida,* or *All's Well That Ends Well,* we must consider "not only the degree of unification of all the elements into a 'unity of sentiment', but the quality and kind of the emotions to be unified, and the elaborateness of the pattern of unification."[34]

This extension of the Aristotelian "unity" leads to the transcending of the Aristotelian notion of types—of tragedy and comedy as distinct species of mimetic poetry. Eliot's argument is that the historical origin of these forms in Greek ritual gives them merely a local, not a permanent, validity—or gives them only one kind of universality. It is to Johnson's credit as a critic, Eliot says, that, though he did not know of the origin of tragedy and comedy in Greek ritual, he "perceived, though not explicitly, that the distinctions of tragic and comic are superficial—for *us.*" Johnson, Eliot goes on,

> is quite aware that the alternation of "tragic" and "comic" [in Shakespeare] is something more than an alternation; he perceives that something different and new is produced. "The interchanges of mingled scenes seldom fail to produce the intended vicissitudes of passion". *"Through all these denominations of the drama Shakespeare's mode of composition is the same."*[35]

Johnson, it will be recalled, defends Shakespeare's practice of mixing comic and tragic scenes. "It is objected," he says, "that by this change of scenes the passions are interrupted in their progression, and that the principal event, being not advanced by a due gradation of preparatory incidents, wants at last the power to move, which constitutes the perfection of dramatick poetry." But, Johnson replies, "The interchanges of mingled scenes seldom fail to produce the intended vicissitudes of passion."[36] Johnson's point here, it would seem, is that Shakespeare interchanges grave and comic scenes because his intention is to produce an interchange of sorrow and laughter, and, what is more, that he commonly succeeds. Johnson argues that there is no psychological reason, as daily experience testifies, why the means Shakespeare employs should not produce the effect he intends, and that the variety of emotion which the plays produce enhances rather than diminishes our pleasure.

"The players," Johnson says, "who in their edition divided our authour's works into comedies, histories, and tragedies, seem not to have distinguished the three kinds, by any very exact or definite ideas." His point is that in classifying works as comedies and tragedies the players take no account of the quality of the action: they call a serious action with a happy ending a comedy, and a light action with an unhappy ending a tragedy. They also tend to ignore the criterion of unity of action in distinguishing tragedies from histories—*Antony and Cleopatra,* Johnson thinks, offers little more in the way of unity of action than *Richard II.*[37] The consequence is, Johnson says, that the critics have failed to see the kind of thing they are dealing with in Shakespeare's plays, and hence have judged his work in the light of principles which do not apply to them. Shakespeare's "mode of composition," he says, is the same in all the plays which his editors distinguish as histories, comedies, and trage-

dies. His plays are "compositions of a distinct kind;
exhibiting the real state of sublunary nature"—a
mingled scene of good and evil, joy and sorrow, loss
and gain, in every proportion and combination.

Johnson's comments, Eliot says, suggest these observations:

> For to those who have experienced the full horror
> of life, tragedy is still inadequate. Sophocles felt more of
> it than he could express, when he wrote *Oedipus the
> King;* Shakespeare, when he wrote *Hamlet;* and Shakes-
> peare had the advantage of being able to employ his
> grave-diggers. In the end, horror and laughter may be
> one—only when horror and laughter have become as
> horrible and laughable as they can be;—whatever the
> conscious intention of the authors—you may laugh or
> shudder over *Oedipus* or *Hamlet* or *King Lear*—or both
> at once: then only do you perceive that the aim of the
> comic and the tragic dramatist is the same; they are
> equally serious. . . . What Plato perceived has not been
> noticed by subsequent dramatic critics; the dramatic poet
> uses the conventions of tragic and comic poetry, so far
> as these are the conventions of his day; there is potential
> comedy in Sophocles and potential tragedy in Aristoph-
> anes, and otherwise they would not be such good trage-
> dians or comedians as they are. It might be added that
> when you have comedy and tragedy united in the wrong
> way, or separated in the wrong way, you get sentiment
> or amusement. The distinction between the tragic and the
> comic is an account of the way in which we try to live;
> when we get below it, as in *King Lear,* we have an ac-
> count of the way in which we do live.[38]

The outcome of all this is a view of serious literature which goes beyond Johnson as well as Aristotle.

For Aristotle, and for the Greeks generally, a tragedy, in the broader sense, is an imitation of a serious action —a moral action resulting in happiness or misery. In the narrower sense, the action, besides being serious— having moral or human significance—must be composed of incidents which have the special power of exciting pity and fear. Later critics generally adopt the broader of these views, regarding drama as the mirror of life. Thus Dryden's working description of a play is *"a just and lively image of human nature, representing its passions and humours, and the changes of fortune to which it is subject, for the delight and instruction of mankind."* And this is substantially the view of Johnson, for whom a play exhibits "the real state of sublunary nature," "those general passions and principles by which all minds are agitated and the whole system of life is continued in motion."[39]

Eliot's view of serious literature resembles that of the Middle Ages. Medieval writers have little understanding of comedy and tragedy in what Johnson calls "the rigorous and critical sense." Indeed, what Johnson says of Shakespeare's first editors—that they ignore the quality of action and distinguish comedy from tragedy solely in terms of happy and unhappy endings—is true of the Middle Ages. It is true, for instance, of the definitions of tragedy and comedy which Dante offers in his letter to Can Grande. But Dante, a professed Aristotelian, treats of poetry largely after the fashion of Horace and the Romans generally—that is to say, rhetorically. And yet that is not altogether true. His poetics of the canzone is in effect a theory of lyric poetry considered as a form of discourse. And with

Dante the lyric embraces "the whole of the art of poetic song," and that includes what he understands by comic and tragic poetry. To Dante, tragedians and comedians are simply poets. He calls the highest style of poetry the "tragic." Such poetry—Virgil's *Aeneid* is an instance—deals with the worthiest subjects: war, love, and virtue. As for the *Commedia,* the subject, he says, "taken allegorically, is man"—man considered in the light of theological morality.[40]

Eliot is in spirit perhaps no less an Aristotelian than Dante, though his recasting of Aristotle is adjusted to the course of modern thought about literary art. What this course is he indicates in his essay on "Shakespearian Criticism." First, there is the distinction between poetry and drama. "The attention of the eighteenth-century critic in England," he says, "is rather on the poetry than the drama." By the nineteenth century the plays of Shakespeare have become "dramatic poems to be read, rather than plays to be seen." Secondly, there is the assimilation of poetry to philosophy. The chief agents of this development are the German Romantic critics. Of these last Eliot says:

> Neglecting the circumstances in which the plays were written . . . and paying little attention to their dramatic merits, the Germans concentrated their attention chiefly upon the philosophical significance of character. They penetrate to a deeper level than that of the simple moral values attributed to great literature by earlier times, and foreshadow the "criticism of life" definition by Arnold.

Coleridge is the most notable English representative of this movement.

But when Coleridge released the truth that Shakespeare already in *Venus and Adonis* and *Lucrece* gave proof of "a most profound, energetic and *philosophic* mind" he was perfectly right, if we use these adjectives rightly, but he supplied a dangerous stimulant to the more adventurous. "Philosophic" is of course not the right word, but it cannot simply be erased: you must find another word to put in its place, and the word has not yet been found. The sense of the profundity of Shakespeare's "thought", or of his thinking-in-images, has so oppressed some critics that they have been forced to explain themselves by unintelligibles.

The German critics and Coleridge, Eliot observes, "by their criticism of Shakespeare, radically altered the reflective attitude of criticism towards poetry."[41]

The change, it may be said, reflects the thought and feeling of the time. Shakespeare was regarded as a modern—a Romantic—writer. Critics found in his works an import which did not seem to be explicable in terms of classical or neo-classical poetics. It went beyond a just representation of human action and passion as determined by moral and psychological truth. It had, it seemed, a philosophic significance. Moreover, poetry—art in general—became an object of philosophic analysis. And the change in literary criticism is connected, as both cause and effect, with the development of modern philosophic aesthetics.

Speaking of Johnson as a critic, Eliot says that "we cannot say whether to classify him as the last of one kind or the first of another." Johnson, that is, represents both the criticism which is based on poetic genres and the concept of imitation and that which is concerned not so much with the kinds of poetry as with the nature and function of poetry itself. He thus reflects, to a degree, the tendency of his age to speculate about the place of poetry in the general context of life, a tendency culminating in Kant's *Critique of Judgment*, which, it may be said, marks the start of modern philosophic aesthetics.

Johnson's appeal, in defending Shakespeare, "from criticism to nature" is a sign of the times in both criticism and philosophy. The age turns away from the conventional and arbitrary in literature and social institutions to search for the principles which are explanatory of human behavior in all its forms. These principles it finds in the psychological analysis of the forms and operations of the mind, and it applies its principles to knowledge, morals, religion, and art.

The psychological method as applied to art begins not with the work of art, but with the behavior of the artist or the person enjoying art. In England and France, the key to art is sought in the psychological analysis of taste and beauty. In the view of a representative thinker like Hume, taste is not a judgment of the reason, based on abstract, a priori principles; it is a judgment of feeling and imagination. Though, when taste is valid, the feeling is relative to the forms and qualities of works of art, beauty is not a quality in objects, but exists merely in the feeling of the person contemplating objects. This feeling is one of immediate pleasure, valuable in itself. Yet, in the last analysis, its value, like that of other feelings, is derived from the principle of utility, the satisfaction of a sensuous or moral interest.[42]

For Hume, then, criticism is not a science. It is concerned with beauty, which is something felt, not perceived—feeling is not a determination of external fact. We can indeed make the feeling itself an object of inquiry and reason about it, but in that case we are dealing with a new fact, one among the other facts of human behavior;[43] and with Hume all such facts are explicable in terms of the mechanism of sensations and impressions. Thus taste or beauty is merely a branch of psychology, or, as Hume has it, moral philosophy.

It is Baumgarten,[44] we are told, who first gives the name "aesthetics" to the study of taste and beauty, and it is he, too, who first speaks of this study as a science — a species of knowledge. Baumgarten began with the distinction (handed down in German philosophy from Leibniz through Wolff) between clear and confused knowledge.[45] Clear knowledge meant the logical analysis of things into their determining elements, and confused knowledge the apprehension of objects by sense and feeling. This last is the sphere of aesthetics, which Baumgarten regards as the analogue of logic. His definition is: "Aesthetics (the theory of the fine arts, the theory of the lower kind of knowledge, the art of thinking beautifully, the art of analogical reasoning) is the science of sensuous knowledge." Aesthetics thus designates a mode of sensible thought or knowledge. It is knowledge in the form of sensation and feeling, irreducible and independent. It has its own rationale, which is based on the notion of sensible form. Such form displays a rule, an order of parts, a unity. The perfection of sensible knowledge, according to Baumgarten, is beauty; and beauty is the sense or feeling of the harmony of parts in a sensible form. Beauty is thus the analogue of the rule and order exhibited in logical knowledge. But logical knowledge, or the truth it represents, is not the standard of beauty; for beauty is not truth, nor is it reducible to logic. The standard of beauty is the idea of perfection. And this idea is revealed in nature, in the sensible world, conceived as a harmony of parts. The artist who imitates nature thus imitates in a particular sensible form the idea of perfection exemplified in the organization of the physical world.[46]

CHAPTER 3 KANT

KANT, IN A NOTE in the *Critique of Pure Reason*,[47] observes that "the Germans are the only people who at present (1781) use the word *aesthetic* for what others call criticism of taste." They did so, he says, in the "false hope," first conceived by Baumgarten, of raising the rules of taste to the status of a science. Viewing such efforts as misguided, Kant deprecates the use of "aesthetic" to denote a science of taste and suggests that the term be applied to a doctrine which is a science. It would be advisable, he thinks, to apply the term to the theory of sensibility, in both its transcendental and psychological aspects. This usage, he says, would approximate that of the ancients, who distinguished between sense perception and intellect—*aistheta* and *noeta*.[48]

At the time of this note—nine years before the publication of the *Critique of Judgment*[49]—Kant's view of taste and beauty was closer to Hume's than to Baumgarten's. In 1781 Kant thought that the rules of taste were, and could be nothing more than, empirical; and with Kant empirical rules, not being universal and necessary, did not constitute a true science[50]— that is, philosophic knowledge. Kant held philosophy to be coextensive with the analysis of the a priori principles of experience, and in 1781 he had not yet investigated the a priori principles which, as he was to argue nine years later, bring aesthetic judgment within the scope of a philosophic critique.[51]

In the *Critique of Pure Reason*, he expounds the a priori principles of understanding, the concepts by which mathematics and physics obtain their knowledge of physical nature; in the *Critique of Practical Reason*, he goes on to deal with the a priori principles of reason, which give direction to the will. The understanding is the faculty of theoretical (scientific) knowledge, and the practical reason the faculty of moral ideas. In the *Critique of Judgment*, he turns his attention to the third cognitive faculty, that of judgment, considering under this the special faculty of taste, which is the faculty of aesthetic judgment. Since judgment is a cognitive faculty, it must, Kant argues, have its own a priori principles, which give the rule to a special province of experience—the aesthetic as distinguished from the scientific and the moral.[52]

What gives aesthetic judgment its intellectual significance, then, is that it is subject to a priori principles; and the object of Kant's *Critique* is "to develop and justify the subjective principle of taste, as an *a priori* principle of the judgment."[53] This, according to Kant, is one kind of critique of taste—the philosophic. The other kind is the criticism of works of art. This last is not a science, but an art—it is a skill, not a species of knowledge. Kant's position is that there neither is nor can be a science of taste in the sense of objective rules or criteria in the light of which one might judge a work as beautiful. Taste, he holds, is a judgment of feeling, not a logical judgment—it is not a judgment involving concepts.

Even philosophers of reputation,[54] Kant says, make the error of taking a logical judgment for an aesthetic one. Thus for Baumgarten the standard of beauty is the idea of perfection; and the judgment that a given sensible form is beautiful is made in the light of that idea. According to this view, when we say a rose is beautiful, we mean that the form satisfies the concept of what a rose should be. Our satisfaction comes through thinking of the form of the rose in relation to its concept. Baumgarten calls such a judgment aesthetic, not logical, because it is sensory and confused, not abstract and clear. Kant's point is that the judgment is nonetheless logical for being confused, since it is a judgment according to a concept.

With Kant, then, criticism is not a science, but a skill. Since taste is a matter of feeling, it does not admit of proof. The judgment of taste rests on the immediate delight in an object. It is not a delight which comes through thinking the object; the delight is in the form alone, apart from any underlying concept of what the object is. Accordingly, no one who does not take delight in an object can be reasoned into doing so. It is idle to say to a person who takes no pleasure in a rose:

Roses are beautiful, and therefore this rose is beautiful. So, too, a student who is indifferent to Shakespeare is right in ignoring the teacher who says: Though you may not care for Shakespeare, educated people agree that he is a great poet. All this is nothing, and should be nothing, to the student who takes no direct pleasure in Shakespeare's work. Of course, it might lead such a student to question his taste. A person can rectify and extend his taste. And that is the end which criticism has in view. But taste cannot be taught in the way that a science can. There is a regular procedure for acquiring a knowledge of chemistry, but there is no such procedure for recognizing beauty in a work of art. That is partly what Kant means when he says that taste is aesthetic, not logical.[55]

Criticism, then, is not concerned with premises and proof. Its art or skill consists in illustrating by the analysis of examples the synthesis of thought and image—the imaginative unity—which is the form of the feeling of beauty. This is also the procedure in teaching students of painting or music or writing. For one does not teach a fine art by principles; one teaches it by the critical analysis of examples. The propaedeutic to fine art, Kant says, lies not in precepts, but in a sound education in the humanities.[56]

The usage respecting "aesthetic" which Kant recommends in the note in the *Critique of Pure Reason* is a description of his practice in that work. There aesthetic is "the science of the rules of sensibility in general," and logic is "the science of the rules of understanding in general." Aesthetic, as the science of sensi-

bility, treats of sense perception, the elements of which
are sensation and the a priori forms of space and time.
Understanding, on the other hand, is the power of
thought, and thinking is the act of referring concepts
to perceptions and to other concepts. Understanding,
like sensibility, has its a priori forms, the Categories.
Perception, which depends on sensation, is always sensuous; and understanding, which thinks the objects of
sensuous perception, is always intellectual. Though
one without the other is nothing—blind or empty—
their functions are not interchangeable. "The understanding cannot see, the senses cannot think." These
two powers, Kant says, "should always be carefully
separated and distinguished, and we have therefore
divided the science of the rules of sensibility in general, i.e. aesthetic, from the science of the rules of the
understanding in general, i.e. logic."[57]

Sensibility, which furnishes perceptions, and understanding, which furnishes concepts, are two of the
three elements necessary for experience; the third is
imagination, which serves as a link between sensibility
and understanding. Imagination, too, is both a priori[58]
and empirical—productive and reproductive. The a
priori imagination, like the empirical, is a function of
sensibility. It is a power of synthesis which converts the
data of the senses into images; images, in turn, stimulate the understanding; and the understanding effects
a still higher synthesis by bringing images under concepts. The imagination, it may be said, prepares the
data of the senses in a form which enables the understanding to think them.

Experience is thus an activity of synthesis: the a priori forms of space and time arrange sense-impressions

in spatial and temporal order; the productive imagination organizes the particular perceptions of the senses into images, which are complex unities; and the understanding, acting through concepts, reduces sensible unities to intellectual ones.

In the *Critique of Pure Reason*, Kant arrives at his doctrine of transcendental aesthetic—the a priori forms of space and time—by abstracting from experience all that is contributed by thought, and then by abstracting from sensibility all that goes with sensation. In the *Critique of Judgment*, his procedure is again that of abstraction, but here he is concerned with aesthetics not as a science, but as taste, which is the faculty of judging beauty.

In the *Critique of Judgment*, he begins with a general distinction between subjective and objective:

> That which in the representation of an object is merely subjective, i.e. which decides its reference to the subject, not to the object, is its aesthetical character; but that which serves or can be used for the determination of the object (for cognition) is its logical validity. In the cognition of an object of sense, both references present themselves.[59]

Having distinguished subjective and objective, he then abstracts from the subjective side the elements which have objective reference, and hence play a part in the logical cognition of objects. Thus space, as an a priori form, is necessary to perception, and therefore to thought, which works with the objects of perception. So, too, sensation has an external side, and hence enters into the logical cognition of objects. What remains is

feeling—pleasure and pain; and this is the only element of sensibility which is incapable of serving as an
ingredient of cognition.

> Given representations in a judgment can be empirical
> (consequently, aesthetical); but the judgment which is
> formed by means of them is logical, provided they are re-
> ferred in the judgment to the object. Conversely, if the
> given representations are rational, but are referred in a
> judgment simply to the subject (to its feeling), the judg-
> ment is so far always aesthetical.[60]

What is referred to feeling is so far aesthetic, and what
is referred to an object is so far logical. Here it is the
reference, not the character of the representation—
image or concept—that is the ground of the distinction. Accordingly, the distinction in the *Critique of
Pure Reason* between sensibility and understanding
becomes here a distinction between subjective and objective, feeling and thought.

According to Kant, the understanding acts through
judgment, and judgment is a discursive act of the mind
relating particulars to universals. Kant divides judgment into two kinds, logical and reflective; and he divides reflective judgment into two species, aesthetic
and teleological.

A logical judgment is determinant. It starts with a
given concept and subsumes a particular under that
concept. In a reflective judgment, the particular is giv-
en, and the concept under which it is thought has to
be supplied. What makes reflective judgment possible
is the principle of purpose or ends. This is an a priori
subjective principle. That is to say, it is not, like caus-

ality, a principle which serves for the logical cognition of external objects, nor is it, like the categorical imperative, a principle which serves to determine the will—it is a principle neither of nature nor of freedom. It is simply a guide for thought, a point of view which is natural to the human mind and which enables the mind to make intelligible to itself things which otherwise would remain unintelligible.[61]

The notion of purpose is derived from the will. According to Kant, the will, regarded as the faculty of desire, is one of "the natural causes in the world, viz. that cause which acts in accordance with concepts." Purpose or end, then, is the effect brought about or determined by the concept of the effect. Thus the concept of a flowerpot, as entertained by a potter, is the cause of the flowerpot (or of its possibility), the flowerpot being the purpose or end of the concept. On the other hand, the existence or possibility of a rose is the effect of mechanism—the interaction of its parts. If, however, we think of the rose as the effect of a concept of the rose, apart from a will, we are thinking of a purpose without purpose.[62]

The teleological view assumes that the objects of nature are the outcome of concepts working in nature. It regards the parts of a rose as dependent on the concept of the rose—as though the whole came before the parts. The use of this hypothesis is that it enables one to render intelligible to oneself the function and organization of the parts of the rose. In a teleological judgment, the form of the rose—its attributes—is referred to the concept of what sort of thing a rose is to be. This is very much like an ordinary logical judgment, except that the concept it employs is subjective, not objective, and hence it does not result in a theoretical cognition of roses. But, since the hypothesis leads to such cognitions, teleological judgments are a part of theoretical philosophy.[63]

When the existence or possibility of a thing is regarded as the outcome of a concept of the thing, we have what Kant calls "a representation of objective purpose." In an aesthetic judgment, however, we have "a representation of formal or subjective purpose." The form of an object, instead of being referred to the concept of the object, is referred to the feeling of the subject, so that feeling, not a concept, is the predicate of the judgment. Here the form of the object, apart from any concept of what sort of thing the object is to be, is the cause of the feeling of pleasure, which is the effect—the purpose or end—of the form. It is as if the form were designed with this effect in view, but no underlying concept is involved, and no concept is produced. The contemplation of the form results in pleasure, and the pleasure leads to a renewal of contemplation, the consequence being an intensification of the aesthetic state of mind; and this self-maintaining activity is its own end—what Kant calls the "subjective purpose" of the form.[64]

Though this account of subjective purpose is incomplete, it will do for the present. An aesthetic judgment, then, is a judgment according to subjective purpose. In such a judgment, the form of the object (apart from a concept and apart from desire) is referred to the feeling of the subject, the feeling of pleasure or displeasure being the basis of the judgment. The judgment is an expression of pleasure in the form of the object, or, what is the same thing, a judgment of beauty. Such a judgment is disinterested: the pleasure it expresses is independent of desire and the existence of the object. It is also universal: the pleasure is valid for everyone. Lastly, it is necessary: the pleasure is the consequence of a judgment directed to the form of the object.

Kant calls a judgment which satisfies these conditions a pure aesthetic judgment, or a pure judgment of taste; he also speaks of it as a free judgment. Both terms, "pure" and "free," mean that the judgment is a priori or transcendental, not empirical or psychological. It is a judgment in which abstraction is made from everything empirical or practical. Kant distinguished two species of practical judgments, sensuous and moral. The first is based on sensation—desire apart from concepts; the second is based on desire mediated by concepts—desire having a reference to objective purpose, to some good. What is common to both these species of practical judgment is that they involve "interest"—desire and the existence of objects and actions which excite desire. Since "interest," whether of sense or of reason, varies with the physical constitution and the character of the subject, judgments based on "interest" are private and partial, not universal and necessary.

Kant elucidates the notion of a pure judgment of taste by contrasting it with sensuous and moral judgments. As has been said, in the general sense, the reference of any representation—image or concept— to feeling is so far aesthetic—that is, subjective, not objective. But the pleasure which is based on sensation or on the idea of good is not pure—is not, that is to say, beauty. Kant distinguishes three kinds of pleasure: the gratification of sense and emotion—the pleasant; the satisfaction of moral feeling—the good; and the reflective judgment of form—beauty.

A sensuous judgment is a judgment of sense—the gratification afforded by the fragrance of a rose or the dryness of a wine. Such judgments are private. No one quarrels about them, seriously. In spite of a certain measure of empirical agreement, there is no rule which applies to them. A man and wife, one preferring dry wine and the other sweet, can by exercising forbearance live in logical harmony. Similarly, in a painting, the element of sense is represented by color; and in music by tone. A judgment based on the gratification afforded by these elements is not, according to Kant, pure, a pure judgment being concerned solely with form, in the one case with design and in the other with composition. Color and tone do indeed enter into taste as contributory elements, for, by making design and composition definite and precise, they facilitate the intuition of form. But the pleasant feeling, the charm, which attaches to the variety and contrast of color and of tone is not beauty, and to take it for beauty is the corruption of taste.[65]

The same objection applies to judgments based on the gratification of emotion.[66] We are, in general, pleased or pained by whatever, in fancy or actuality, agrees or disagrees with our moods and impulses, our emotional predispositions. Thus one person approves of a painting which depicts a country lane because it stirs a pleasant memory; another dislikes Gothic cathedrals because he disbelieves in religion; another enjoys a novel because it deals with romantic love; and still another judges a play to be poor because it represents vulgar people sympathetically. All such judgments are "interested," and hence they are as little subject to criticism as those based on physical sensation. In such matters, everyone has his own taste, which is irrelevant to the aesthetic judgment of beauty.

So the satisfaction we take in judgments based on the idea of good—perfection—is also "interested." For one thing, such judgments, since they depend on concepts, are not aesthetic, but logical. Kant calls the beauty they judge—the agreement of a form with its idea— "dependent" beauty, which is quite a different thing from aesthetic beauty. In the second place, such judgments are disqualified because they are "interested." They depend on the concept of a purpose, and hence involve the relation of reason to desire and of desire to the existence of objects.[67]

"Everything practical," Kant says, "so far as it contains motives, has reference to sentiments, and these belong to empirical sources of knowledge."[68] Empirical judgments are egoistic: they are based on the interest of the self, on what furthers or hinders its well-being. Further, such judgments are expressions merely of private feeling, and private joys and griefs are not in themselves aesthetic. Their significance is not philosophic, but psychological and practical, social and historical—they are a part of what Kant calls "empirical anthropology." To be sure, judgments based on private feeling obtain a certain measure of conventional agreement. It is possible through inductive generalization to establish an empirical standard of taste. But such a standard is binding on no one, for it is neither universal nor necessary. If the egoistic

sensibility is to be the standard of taste, every inde-
pendent-minded person will, and ought to, make his
own feeling of well-being the basis of his judgment.
But self-satisfaction is not beauty; and, if all satisfaction is reducible to self-satisfaction, beauty is a mere
word, not a reality.

> If, then, the judgment of taste is not to be valid merely
> *egoistically*, but according to its inner nature—i.e. on ac-
> count of itself, and not on account of the examples
> that others give of their taste—to be necessarily
> valid *pluralistically*, if we regard it as a judgment
> which may exact the adhesion of everyone, then
> there must lie at its basis some *a priori* principle
> (whether objective or subjective) to which we can never
> attain by seeking out the empirical laws of mental
> changes. For these only enable us to know how we judge,
> but do not prescribe to us how we ought to judge. . . .
> Thus the empirical exposition of aesthetical judgments
> may be a beginning of a collection of materials for a
> higher investigation; but a transcendental discussion of
> this faculty is also possible, and it is an essential part
> of the "Critique of Taste." For if it had not *a priori*
> principles, it could not possibly pass sentence on the
> judgment of others, and it could not approve or blame
> them with any appearance of right.[69]

This passage is preceded by a comment on Burke's
On the Sublime and Beautiful, of which Kant held a
high opinion. "As psychological observations," he says,
"these analyses of the phenomena of our mind are ex-
ceedingly beautiful and afford rich material for the
favorite investigations of empirical anthropology." He
doubtless has in mind also Hume's "Of the Standard

of Taste," which says what there is to say in general
on the empirical theory of taste.

Hume's position may be described as relativism
moderated, more or less, by empirical agreement. According to Hume, though feeling is private, and the
variety of feeling is even greater in fact than in appearance, there is, up to a point, a standard of taste.
Its foundation is the observations drawn from established models and the uniformity of psychological
laws in respect to what pleases and displeases. But,
since such laws, though uniform, are diverse in operation, "the true standard of taste and beauty" is the
joint verdict of critics qualified by sensibility, intelligence, knowledge, and experience of art. Still, even
among qualified critics, diversity of temperament and
character and of time and place creates differences of
judgment for which no standard exists by which they
can be decided. Hume thus advances and retreats. In
one passage he intimates that what qualified critics
do is "establish their own sentiment as the standard of beauty." On the other hand, we must hold "a
true and decisive standard to exist somewhere, to wit,
real existence and matter of fact." He seems to mean
that the true critic is "a man in general," a man liberated from his "individual being" and his "peculiar
circumstances."

Though Kant does not speak of Hume in this connection, it is just at this point, according to Kant, that
psychological exposition must be supplemented and
corrected by philosophic analysis. Kant observes that
when we talk of beauty we do in fact expect others to
agree with us, though we make no such claim in respect to our private enjoyments; and this at least sug-

gests that beauty is universal and necessary. For instance, we speak of beauty as though it were a property of objects, something outside ourselves. Though beauty is indeed a feeling, it is nevertheless universal and necessary. And therein we uncover, says Kant, a "strange and irregular" fact about aesthetic judgment. For so far as logicians know, only theoretical judgments—logical judgments of objective phenomena— are universal and necessary. But here is a judgment based on feeling, a singular judgment, which is yet universal and necessary. True, such a judgment is an ideal; but if we can demonstrate that it is possible, we shall have obtained a footing in the world for beauty.

What makes it possible is the a priori principle of subjective purpose, the exposition of which may now be completed. In a judgment according to subjective purpose, the form of an object is referred to feeling, pleasure or pain being the ground of the judgment. We are not to think, however, that the form is the cause and the pleasure the effect, as if the one were directly dependent on the other, as in a simple instance of stimulus-response. What happens rather is that the form excites a harmony of imagination and understanding—the cognitive faculties—and the feeling is referred to this harmony. The pleasure is the consciousness of the harmony of imagination and understanding which is excited by the form. This harmony is not an objective relation, which involves the reference of a particular to a concept; it is internal or subjective. Therefore, it cannot be thought; it can only be felt. The judgment, being based on feeling, is not intellectual, but aesthetic.

Abstraction having been made from sense and concept, the elements involved in the judgment are the form, the cognitive faculties, and feeling. The feeling, which is the basis of the judgment, is the effect of the harmony of imagination and understanding as related to the form. In consequence of this harmony, occasioned by the form and known by feeling, we experience the form as beauty—that is, as a feeling of pleasure which is "disinterested," and hence universal and necessary.

The aesthetic fact is a feeling of pleasure. The critical judgment is that the pleasure is a state of mind excited by the form in abstraction from sense and concept. The philosophic explanation is that the pleasure in form presupposes a harmony of the cognitive faculties. These last, or their mutual accord, function as the middle term, the universal element, in aesthetic judgment. Their function is analagous to that of concepts in intellectual judgments. Thus in a judgment according to subjective purpose, a given form is subsumed under, or referred to, the harmony of the cognitive faculties.

The harmony of the cognitive faculties is, then, the a priori subjective condition which is constitutive of aesthetic judgment. Again, the mutual accord of these faculties is the prerequisite of cognition in general. As we have seen, in order for cognition to take place, the imagination must synthesize the intuitions of sense, and the image thus produced must stimulate the understanding to think the image under a concept and to combine other concepts with this concept. Cognition, then, and the communication of cognition, presupposes a harmony of the cognitive faculties. And this general condition is presupposed in beauty. Thus the accord of the cognitive faculties, though in a different adjustment according to whether the judgment is intellectual or aesthetic, is the subjective condition presupposed in the experience of all men.[70]

It follows that, since the ground of the pleasure in beauty is universal, the pleasure is valid for everyone. The pleasure is also necessary. The necessity, however, is conditional and exemplary. The notion is that whoever judges properly—abstracts from sense and concept and refers the form to the play of the cognitive faculties—ought, as a consequence, to find satisfaction in beauty. And the reason is that the sense of beauty—taste—is a common sense—if not actually at least potentially. The feeling which is the basis of judgment is the effect of the harmony of the cognitive faculties; and this feeling, as has been said, is implicit in every cognition. It is therefore not a private feeling, but common to all. My judgment of taste, then, is an example of a judgment based on a feeling which I share with everyone; and hence I have a right to expect that others who satisfy the conditions of an aesthetic judgment will take a like pleasure in beauty. And this is what is actually presupposed in the discussion of art. The common feeling is, to be sure, an ideal norm. We cannot formulate a rule which shall determine the judgment of taste. All we can do is to say that whoever judges properly *ought* to find satisfaction in beauty.[71]

The key to the *Critique*, according to Kant, is that the pleasure does not precede, but follows, the judgment. We do not say: This pleases me, and therefore it is beautiful. On the contrary, we judge a given form to be beautiful, and our pleasure is the consequence

of the judgment. If all that a judgment of taste assert-
ed was that a given form gave us pleasure, it would be
in the same case as a judgment of sense. For that a
particular form should give us pleasure cannot be determined a priori; a causal relation of this kind can be
known only a posteriori. It is empirical. For instance,
we learn that a certain liquid pleases the palate, and
we compare the liquid in this respect with other li-
quids of the same kind, and we infer that wine is pleas-
ing to the palate. This is a logical judgment based on
empirical fact. If the pleasure in form preceded the
judgment of form, it would be neither universal nor
necessary. In this respect, an aesthetic judgment is similar to a moral judgment; for the satisfaction of moral
feeling does not precede, but follows, the judgment of
reason. The difference is that in aesthetics we judge
apart from concepts.

Aesthetic judgment is a paradox. The basis of the
judgment is feeling, not a concept; yet the feeling is
related to the cognitive faculties. That is to say, there
is a *judgment,* which is *an act of thought,* and this precedes the pleasure. The judgment (thought) is reflective (noncognitive): the form is referred not to a
concept, but to the cognitive faculties, which constitute the a priori subjective condition of the judgment.
We are judging our state of mind (the harmony of
imagination and understanding) as related to the
form of an object. To do this, we must abstract from
sensation and concept and judge that our feeling is
the consequence of our contemplating the form. In
short, we must *think* without concepts if we are to experience the delight of beauty. In aesthetics the sensi-

bility is affected through the intellect acting without concepts.

Aesthetic sensibility, then, is a function of the cognitive faculties—understanding as well as imagination. Knowledge is one effect of the mutual working of these faculties, and beauty is another. Beauty, like knowledge and morality, has its roots in the nature of man as a rational animal. "Pleasantness," says Kant, "concerns irrational animals also, but beauty only concerns men, i.e. animal, but still rational, beings—not merely *quâ* rational (e.g. spirits), but *quâ* animal also—and the good concerns every rational being in general."[72] Beauty, unlike sense and moral reason, is "disinterested," and hence free of the compulsion of desire and duty. In this respect, beauty is like theoretical knowledge. But in aesthetics, though not in science, the working of the cognitive faculties has a *direct* bearing on sensibility.[73] Man, as man, is thus provided with a faculty for evaluating things, not according to desire or reason, but simply according to the free pleasure which is beauty. And this is a human standard of value.[74]

Taste is the sense of beauty. It is the faculty of judging the state of mind, as pleasure or displeasure, which is communicated by a work of art (or nature). And this state of mind, or feeling of pleasure, is the effect of a purely imaginative impression—that is, the direct impression evoked by the intuition of a given form as a unity apart from the concept of an end or purpose. The state of mind is explicable, according to Kant, in terms of the relation of imagination and understanding considered as a priori faculties. The task of a philosophic critique is to formulate the part played by these faculties and their reciprocal relations, and to do this not by psychological analysis, but by analysis based on the conditions of cognition in general.[75]

The relation which defines the aesthetic state of mind is "the imagination's free conformity to law"; or it is the harmony of "the imagination in its *freedom* and the understanding with its *conformity to law*."[76] The reference is not to the reproductive (empirical) imagination, for that, as subject to the laws of association, is not free. And a work which is the product simply of the reproductive imagination is not a manifestation of beauty. What is meant is the a priori imagination, the synthetic faculty as spontaneous and productive of forms which, as we shall see, are expressive of an import other than the historical (empirical) circumstances of life. This imagination, again, is not free if it works according to a concept of an end, for then the form it produces is determined by the concept of what sort of thing the object ought to be; and the judgment in such a case, as we have seen, is a judgment not of taste, but of the good (perfection). If the imagination is to be free, it must be unconditioned by the empirical laws of association or by the a priori schematization of concepts.[77] Yet the free imagination is not unregulated—is not disorderly and incoherent. The regulation is the work of the understanding operating without concepts. It is negative only. The imagination, though free, must not synthesize elements which are inconsistent. Thus the "imagination's free conformity to law" is Kant's formulation of the principle of imaginative unity.

There are two general principles of composition, scientific and aesthetic. The first proceeds by concepts and logic. The second is imaginative: the form is the outcome of feeling regulated by the principle of contradiction,[78] which is the general though negative law of the understanding. This last serves as a kind of tether to the imagination; it leaves the imagination free while keeping it within the limits of intelligibility.

Science requires brains, and art genius.[79] These are quite distinct talents. Further, since method can be taught, science is progressive. But art does not progress. Genius gives the "rule" to art, but the "rule" is incapable of formulation; it can only be exemplified in works of art, and it is a new "rule" in every work. The only way for an artist to learn his business is to sail to the city of Byzantium and there to study the monuments of the soul's magnificence. If he *is* an artist, nature's child, he will be moved to perpetuate the spirit of art in new and original works of beauty.

Beauty, on one side, is the object of a judgment of taste, which is a critical faculty; on the other, it is the product of genius, which is a productive (creative) faculty. Though often one or the other is lacking, art requires both taste and genius. Art here means fine art, art that is beautiful; such art is *sui generis*, and hence it is not to be confused with art in the sense of the adaptation of means to ends: for instance, the art of preparing speeches, or lectures, or books on one subject or another. Fine art, art that is imaginative—"poetry"—is not "literature."

There is a secondary notion of taste which is appropriate to "literature," though not to "poetry." This notion is distinct from taste as the judgment of free beauty as well as from genius, the faculty of production, which is the source of "poetry." It may be called dependent taste. We speak of taste in this secondary or dependent sense in connection, say, with the form of a book considered as a vehicle of thought; if the form is an effective vehicle of the thought, we say the book is "beautifully done." The same critical ability (it involves the judgment of a relation) is required in "poetry," but there it is concerned with the free play of imagination and understanding.[80]

Art is ambiguous in its intention. It is not properly the working out of a predetermined scheme, for then the imagination would be under the constraint of the concept or purpose regulating the work. Besides, a work of this kind aims at producing a concept, and hence is didactic. At the same time, art implies a purpose. The intention of the artist is to produce a definite kind of thing, that is, a work of art, with the immediate design of pleasure. Further, the pleasure appeals not to mere sensation, but, as has been said, to reflection, to a mode of cognition (otherwise art would be nothing serious, but merely an entertainment or diversion). And yet this purpose without a purpose cannot be formulated as an objective rule which should serve for the judgment or creation of beauty. The principle of imaginative unity is an indeterminate norm or ideal; it exists only in works of art; and it is different in every work. It is the product of genius, which is the feeling for the free play of imagination under the negative control of understanding, or it is the talent for thinking coherently in images.[81]

Thus far, except for the distinction between critical and productive, genius is hardly distinguishable from taste, and indeed they are similar in respect to their general form—a free and harmonious adjustment of the cognitive faculties. But genius goes deeper than taste, for it is a function of the spirit or soul in a sense in which taste is not. Kant defines genius as "the faculty of aesthetic ideas." A poem, a prose work—or, for that matter, a woman—may be well arranged and elegant (exhibit the virtues of order and style), and yet be without spirit or soul—without beauty. Aesthetically, spirit or soul is "the animating principle of the mind," and this shows itself as "the faculty of presenting *aesthetical ideas*."

> And by an aesthetical idea I understand that representation of the imagination which occasions much thought, without however any definite thought, i.e. any *concept*, being capable of being adequate to it; it consequently cannot be completely compassed and made intelligible by language. We easily see that it is the counterpart (pendant) of a *rational idea*, which conversely is a concept to which no *intuition* (or representation of the imagination) can be adequate.[82]

"The imagination," says Kant, "(as a productive faculty of cognition) is very powerful in creating another nature, as it were, out of the material that actual nature gives it." The material is given in sensation, according to the laws of the empirical imagination; and the productive (a priori) imagination, which is not passive but active, reorganizes the given material, working it up into forms which go beyond what is given in nature. In the creation of such forms, we attain a measure of freedom from empirical necessity. The new forms are constructed "in accordance with analogical laws, but yet also in accordance with principles which occupy a higher place in reason (laws, too, which are just as natural to us as those by which understanding comprehends empirical nature)."

Up to this point, Kant has spoken of beauty in terms of imagination and understanding—of imaginative unity. Now he brings in reason (as distinguished from understanding), the faculty of the supersensible, the source of moral concepts. The a priori principle of reason is that of purpose, subjective in respect to aesthetics, and objective in respect to the good. The term "idea" signifies representations which are non-cognitive (non-theoretical), of which there are two kinds, rational and aesthetic.[83] A rational idea is a moral (intellectual) concept which is in excess of sensible intuition. An aesthetic idea is not a concept; it is "an intuition (of the imagination)" for which no adequate concept can be found. It is called an idea because it is non-cognitive and because it exceeds experience on its conceptual side, as rational ideas exceed it on its sensible side.

Though an intuition of the imagination is not a concept, it is, by virtue of its connection with reason, associated with rational concepts. It approximates, says Kant, "to a presentation of concepts of reason (intellectual ideas), thus giving to the latter the appearance of objective reality." This relation takes several forms. Here are two related forms:

The poet ventures to realize to sense, rational ideas of invisible beings, the kingdom of the blessed, hell, eternity, creation, etc.; or even if he deals with things of which there are examples in experience—e.g. death, envy and all vices, also love, fame, and the like—he tries by means of imagination, which emulates the play of reason in its quest after a maximum [a totality which exceeds sensible perception], to go beyond the limits of experience and to present them to sense with a completeness of which there is no example in nature.[84]

Kant's object, in these examples, is, I take it, simply to make the point that aesthetic ideas (intuitions of the imagination) resemble rational ideas (concepts) in going beyond "the limits of experience." In the second example, the imagination constructs a picture of death, say, which is fuller than any experienced instances of death. It thus emulates reason, which thinks totalities that are incomprehensible to the senses. Kant, it would appear, is thinking here of the imagination which is operative in cognition; for he says, in connection with these two examples, that the faculty of aesthetic ideas, "considered in itself, is properly only a talent (of the imagination)." It is perhaps the imagination considered apart from reason.

At any rate, here is a description of imagination which is creative:

If now we place under a concept a representation of the imagination belonging to its presentation, but which occasions in itself more thought than can ever be comprehended in a definite concept and which consequently aesthetically enlarges the concept itself in an unbounded fashion, the imagination is here creative, and it brings the faculty of intellectual ideas (the reason) into movement; i.e. by a representation more thought (which indeed belongs to the concept of the object) is occasioned than can in it be grasped or made clear.[85]

In this, as in the first two examples, the imaginative form is regarded as a presentation of a concept, the difference being that in the last example the intuition of the imagination stirs the mind (reason) at a deeper level.

Kant offers still another version of aesthetic ideas. In this version the form is regarded not as a presentation of a concept, but merely as an imaginative attribute of it. Some objects, like "the sublimity and majesty of creation," have no adequate sensible embodiment, and can be represented only approximately by imaginative attributes. "Thus Jupiter's eagle with the lightning in its claws is an attribute of the mighty king of heaven, as the peacock is of his magnificent queen." This is not in itself a very interesting example of poetry, but the principle Kant sees in it has its importance. He says of aesthetic attributes:

They do not, like *logical attributes,* represent what lies in our concepts of the sublimity and majesty of creation, but something different, which gives occasion to the imagination to spread itself over a number of kindred representations that arouse more thought than can be expressed in a concept determined by words. They furnish an *aesthetical idea,* which for that rational idea takes the place of logical presentation; and thus, as their proper office, they enliven the mind by opening out to it the prospect into an illimitable field of kindred representations.[86]

The principle is the essential principle of poetry, the faculty of aesthetic ideas: "an intuition (of the imagination) for which an adequate concept can never be found." And the importance of the principle is that "poetry," so defined, is not confined to verse.

> But beautiful art does this not only in the case of painting or sculpture (in which the term "attribute" is commonly employed); poetry and rhetoric also get the spirit that animates their works simply from the aesthetical attributes of the object, which accompany the logical and stimulate the imagination, so that it thinks more by their aid, although in an undeveloped way, than could be comprehended in a concept and therefore in a definite form of words.[87]

Here is an instance of a rational idea quickened by an aesthetic attribute:

> When the great King in one of his poems expresses himself as follows:
>> Oui, finisson sans trouble et mourons sans regrets,
>> En laissant l'univers comblê de nos bienfaits.
>> Ainsi l'astre du jour au bout de sa carriere,
>> Répand sur l'horizon une douce lumière;
>> Et les derniers rayons qu'il darde dans les airs,
>> Sont les derniers soupirs qu'il donne à l'univers;
> he quickens his rational idea of a cosmopolitan disposition at the end of life by an attribute which the imagination (in remembering all the pleasures of a beautiful summer day that are recalled at its close by a serene evening) associates with that representation, and which excites a number of sensations and secondary representations for which no expression is found.[88]

And here is an instance of a sensible representation quickened by an intellectual idea:

> The sun arose
> As calm from virtue springs.

The consciousness of virtue, if we substitute it in our thoughts for a virtuous man, diffuses in the mind a multitude of sublime and restful feelings, and a boundless prospect of a joyful future, to which no expression that is measured by a definite concept completely attains.[89]

It is the idea of the supersensible, Kant says, that here quickens the image, "but only by the aesthetical [element], that subjectively attaches" to the concept —the feeling diffused in the mind.

Kant concludes:

> In a word, the aesthetical idea is a representation of the imagination associated with a given concept, which is bound up with such a multiplicity of partial representations in its free employment that for it no expression marking a definite concept can be found; and such a representation, therefore, adds to a concept much ineffable thought, the feeling of which quickens the cognitive faculties, and with language, which is the mere letter, binds up spirit also.[90]

An aesthetic idea, it may be said, is an imaginative expression—"an internal intuition which the imagination binds up with a given representation." The imagination is a medium or agency (a faculty or power) for expressing in sensuous form an internal intuition. The synthetic activity is the subjective side of imagination, and the form is the objective side. Further, such an expression may be exhibited in a phrase, a verse, or a work as a whole. In poetry, the imaginative form is a synthesis of thought and image. Here thought means concepts—abstractions; and image, the associations evoked by the image—undetermined thought. The interaction of the two is the aesthetic idea or imaginative expression. Again, the poetry is the synthesis, and there are as many "kinds" of poetry as there are modes of synthesis. Thus, for instance, the image may be basic, and the concept may serve to deepen the meaning (or feeling) of the image; or the concept may be basic, and the image may serve to extend the meaning of the concept—in terms of undetermined thought or feeling. In both cases we have poetry[91] so long as there is a synthesis, more or less intense, and so long as the synthesis is expressive of thought which is in excess of logical description, or, what is the same thing, is expressive of the feeling or state of mind implicit in the synthesis.

Genius, as the faculty of aesthetic ideas, is, then, the talent for thinking in images—thinking without determinate concepts, which place the imagination in constraint. And this talent is original. The artistic spirit is exemplified by the principle of imaginative unity, and that principle is new in every work of art.[92] That is what creation means—bringing into existence something which did not exist before. If there were rules for art, as there are for science, we should have no need for genius; anyone with a good head and industry could learn to be an artist. Genius learns what it has to learn only from existing works of art. But what it learns by study and experiment is technique, the instrument of genius. It is taste, the critical faculty, which is here exercised, corrected, and extended. Taste, says Kant, is the discipline or training of genius. But the study of existing works is not the imitation of them. Such works are exemplary in that they awaken in the gifted individual the feeling for the free exercise of his talent. Originality, according to Kant, is not individual peculiarity. It presupposes a knowledge of what has been done as well as the autonomy of the human spirit.[93]

It follows that originality, which is the mark of genius, is essentially impersonal.[94] Impersonality is to genius what disinterestedness is to taste; and both are concerned with what is universal. Judgments based on the gratification of sense and emotion are private, and there is nothing universal in sensation. The production of beauty, no less than the judgment of it, requires detachment from the egoistic sensibility, which is bound by interest and the laws of the reproductive imagination. The productive imagination works up the material of sensation (its joys and griefs) into forms which are quite distinct from empirical fancies. And this is effected, as in taste, by "the operation of reflection." It is thought which is universal (not sensation), and feeling as the consequence of thought.[95] Concepts are objectively universal, but art is not the communication of concepts. Art is the communication of the feeling or state of mind, without the mediation of a concept, which is the consequence of the undetermined thought annexed to or fused with rational ideas. And what makes such communication possible is an imagination unconditioned by determinate concepts or the laws of association, an imagination sustained by the autonomy of the human spirit.

The imagination, with Kant, is not an ultimate faculty. Considered in itself, it is a function of sensibility, relative to the data of sense. As such it is an instrument of cognition as well as a means of gratifying sense and emotion. In this last capacity it offers entertainment and distraction from boredom.[96] True, even the play of sensation is productive of thought by a kind of mechanical association, but here the play of the mind is transitory and aimless, leaving no residue for reflection. This is the general character of popular entertainment. What lends games, for example, the appearance of seriousness is that they enlist the interest of the egoistic sensibility. Victory and defeat carry the imputation of superiority and inferiority, and hence engage the vanity of the ego. Though games excite a vivid play of emotion—hope, fear, joy, anger—they offer merely a physiological exercise, useful for health, but devoid of gain for the spirit.

The imagination becomes a purposive mode of cognition by virtue of its connection with the higher faculties of the mind, understanding and reason. The understanding, exercising negative control, lends the imagination coherence. The understanding, Kant says, is also presupposed in artistic intention, that is, the concept of the work as a definite product.[97] The imagination, however, is not employed in the service of cognition, and its representation is not determined by a definite concept. The artistic intention is effected by the expression of aesthetic ideas, and these have their seat in reason.

It is the connection with reason that explains the seriousness of art. Art is often taken for entertainment, and that indeed is what it appears to be. Poetry, Kant says, "declares itself to be a mere entertaining play of the imagination"; "the *poet* merely promises an entertaining play with ideas, and yet it has the same effect upon the understanding as if he had only intended to carry on its business."[98] At an art gallery—in New York, London, Paris, Amsterdam, the Hague, Munich, Vienna, Florence, Rome—people do make the abstractions Kant speaks of, contemplating the form alone, engaged with the imaginative impression. Sometimes, at a concert, the spirit being dull and heavy, it cannot escape the hold of the empirical imagination, and the mind, instead of following the music, is lost in a train of private images, which offer easy gratification. It takes an effort to shake off the weight of empirical circumstances, and the mind is once again contemplative, serious, as though the musicians were convened to carry on the business of the understanding. Now the mind is fully occupied, content with its activity, and yet no interest is aroused. It is enjoying the free play of the cognitive faculties as related to the music; it is pursuing a purpose without purpose.

Why do we insist that art is important? For we do insist, and, Kant says, exact the assent of others, taking a poor view of those who dissent—trivial people, deficient in soul or spirit. If art is simply a free play of the cognitive faculties, wherein does it differ from entertainment? It is a non-cognitive activity, making no contribution to knowledge. It is not a moral occupation, for art is quite indifferent to duty. Kant, whose philosophy has a strong moral bias, says that people, with the best intentions, who submit everything to a moral standard like to think that an interest in art indicates a good moral character. But the facts, he adds, lend little support to this view, for "connoisseurs in taste" are frequently anything but models of moral deportment. Indeed, some people go so far as to assert that morality and art are incompatible. The fact, Kant says, is that the feeling for the beautiful is specifically different from moral feeling, but that nevertheless the two are not incompatible.[99]

The value we attach to art, then, does not have its basis in man as scientist or in man as moral being. Art, as the production of the beautiful, has its basis in humanity, which is common to all men. The significance of art is that the free play of the cognitive faculties is not mere play; it is expressive of the inmost self, the soul or spirit, of human nature. Genius (the guardian spirit), the faculty of aesthetic ideas, gives the "rule" to art, but it is nature, working through genius, that is the ultimate source of art. And the essence of human nature, in Kant's terms, is reason, the seat of both rational and aesthetic ideas. Reason, in general, is the faculty, and idea, of the supersensible. And the immediate effect of art is to elevate and point the mind in the direction of the supersensible, the region of ideas, the sphere of ineffable thought. It is the import of undetermined thought, or the feeling accompanying it, which fixes the attention and strains the imagination of readers of poetry, viewers of pictures, and auditors of music.

There is something in the state of mind evoked by art which cannot quite be made out—the thing-in-itself, the reality, the "supersensible substrate" of both external and human nature. It lies, as it were, just beyond the horizon of conceptual knowledge. We can think it, as a possibility, but nothing in our perceptual experience quite answers to it. For Kant, there is no intellectual intuition—concepts apart from percepts are empty. On the other hand, the senses in themselves are blind—they cannot think a supersensible idea. The best that art can do—art as the attempt to render rational ideas in sensuous form, art as the expression of aesthetic ideas—is to evoke the ineffable thought or the accompanying feeling of the supersensible.[100]

Reason, the supersensible, is both a mode of thought and the object of thought. It is the idea which man forms of himself as a finite intelligible creature as distinguished from an object implicated in the complex of mechanical laws. He conceives the essence of his nature, as man not animal, to be a principle unconditioned by physical causation, hence a supersensible or intelligible or rational principle. This unconditioned principle is the idea of freedom, which is the essence of humanity. It is the nature of man (his reason is so constituted) to distinguish his humanity from his animality in terms of the unconditioned principle of freedom (the supersensible). As animal, as an organized material being, he is subject to the procedures of organic interaction. In these procedures nature appears as art—art as the adjustment of means to ends. We may, if we like, speak of "natural purposes," but these are not rational ends. They are conditioned effects, material and mechanical. A "natural purpose" is not a distinctly human purpose; for humanity expresses itself in unconditioned purposes. And it is in this sense that humanity is an end in itself.[101]

The supersensible, the unconditioned principle, is an object of thought, but not of knowledge. This follows from Kant's definition of scientific knowledge. We have no intellectual choice, according to Kant, but to reconcile ourselves to the notion that the "intelligible substrate" of life is inscrutable, whatever the grief involved in this disengagement from our fondest metaphysical hopes.

Nevertheless, the idea of the supersensible is for all practical and explanatory purposes indispensable. Human life apart from the idea of purpose is unintelligible; apart from this idea the values distinctive of human life are without a basis, for the supersensible as reason is the source of human purposes. Nor is it only moral (political) and aesthetic values that stand to lose; for, if we give up the idea of purpose, our scientific knowledge of nature remains incomplete. The idea of purpose, then, is presupposed in every sphere of life, though with different application; and for all practical purposes the supersensible is sufficiently determined in experience and explained in terms of the a priori principles which underlie both determined and reflective judgment, including aesthetic judgment.[102]

Thus the universal import of art is explicable only by reference to the idea of humanity (freedom, the supersensible), which is implicit, however obscurely, in both the creation and judgment of art (genius and taste); and that is as far as we can go in the attempt to render the import of art intelligible.[103] If we discard the idea of humanity, as the ultimate explanation of the universality of art, we are left with two mutually contradictory and unacceptable views. On the one hand, we have the empirical position that the judgment of art is, in the end, on the same footing as the judgment of wine. Whatever agreement exists is owing to the accidental similarity of physiological organization and of external conditions of time and place. We should have to consent to Epicurus'[104] dictum that all pleasure is reducible to the gratification of bodily sense, or, in more modern terms, to the organization of impulses or energies—in short, to biological harmony. In the gloom of this view, we cannot see any distinction between "natural" and human purposes and values—between bodily feeling and moral and aesthetic feeling. Again, according to this view, "universality" means the participation in experiences (each in his own way) which have no common basis, a participation made possible by the social existence of works of art. In our time, we observe that the critic, with ritualistic flourishes, offers a "reading," which he says is merely *his* reading, at the same time expecting universal agreement. If the idea of humanity is not constitutive of artistic experience, every critic erects his private feeling into an absolute (the unconditioned), which he enforces as he can, as though taste were founded on objective principles. And that brings us to the second view: that the judgment of taste is based on concepts. According to this view, if there are no objective principles of judgment (criticism), it is idle to quarrel about taste, since no position can be supported by proof; and taste which cannot

be so supported loses all claim to universal assent.
True, says Kant, up to a point. But if taste is based
on objective principles, it is not an aesthetic, but simply a disguised logical, judgment, involving the relation of form to the concept of the object. The consequence is that between these two views, the one
reducing taste to the pleasant and the other to the
good (perfection), beauty is shuffled out of the world,
and all that remains is a mere name, expressing perhaps a mixture of sensuous and moral satisfaction.[105]
The resolution of the antinomy is this: if art is to
have universal import, it must involve a concept, not,
however, a determinate (logical) concept, but an indeterminate one—the rational concept of the supersensible, the "intelligible substrate" of humanity.
This concept offers no knowledge, nor can it supply
proof for the judgment of taste. The reference to this
concept is through imagination (sensuous form),
which points the mind in the direction of the supersensible.
Kant concludes his exposition of ideas thus:

We can consequently explain *genius* as the faculty
of *aesthetical ideas*, by which at the same time is shown
the reason why in the products of genius it is the nature
(of the subject), and not a premeditated purpose, that
gives the rule to the art (of the producion of the beautiful). For since the beautiful must not be judged by concepts, but by the purposive attuning of the imagination
to agreement with the faculty of concepts in general, it
cannot be rule and precept which can serve as the subjective standard of that aesthetical but unconditioned
purposiveness in beautiful art that can rightly claim to
please everyone. It can only be that in the subject which

is nature and cannot be brought under rules of concepts, i.e. the supersensible substrate of all his faculties (to which no concept of the understanding extends), and consequently that with respect to which it is the final purpose given by the intelligible [part] of our nature to harmonize all our cognitive faculties. Thus alone is it possible that there should be *a priori* at the basis of this purposiveness, for which we can prescribe no objective principle, a principle subjective and yet of universal validity.[106]

We may remind ourselves that Kant is engaged in a philosophic analysis of art and beauty—the first such systematic effort; and that means, with Kant, the analysis of the mental powers involved in art. His reference to these powers is to the powers in general, so that his meaning is abstract. But artistic experience, of course, involves empirical detail, the reproductive as well as the a priori or productive imagination.

On the side of taste, the state of mind evoked by a sensuous form exhibiting imaginative unity is a free and harmonious play of imagination and understanding; this state is judged not by a concept, but by feeling; and this feeling is the feeling of what it means to be a human being[107] as against an object implicated in the chain of physical causation—a being detached from the empirical ego (sense and private emotion), an autonomous, self-sustaining, being. On the side of genius, it is human nature, in this universal sense, which is expressed in aesthetic ideas. It is humanity, liberated human nature, speaking through genius, which is the basis of the universal import of art. Art, as involving both taste and genius, is intimate but impersonal. It is humanity *in* the individual, not as

external to him, which speaks in art. The judgment
of taste is a singular judgment of an empirical object
which yet involves a reference to the idea of humanity.
So genius works with the given material of sense and
of time and place, to which it responds in an individual way. But it detaches itself from its egoistic interests as well as from its time and place. It looks out
to the supersensible, and in the light of that vision or
feeling it creates an imaginative form which stands
to the empirically given as a second nature. This transformation is the work of the spirit, the principle of
freedom, which is impersonal. Art is self-expression,
but it is not the empirical self that is expressed; it
is the impersonal or universal self. Art is the revelation of the human spirit.[108]

If art, as the expression of thought and feeling, is its
own end, it may be said that, with Kant, what makes
art possible is that man is a moral being. The artist
must be a free (moral) man before he can be an artist.
The supersensible as reason or freedom is the seat not
only of aesthetic ideas, but, in the first place, of
rational ideas of determinate ends—the moral idea,
the good. Kant, rejecting the metaphysics of realism,
regards man as primarily a moral being, whose essence is freedom and whose ultimate destiny is a life
in society determined by the idea of freedom or
reason. Kant, accordingly, finds the ultimate significance of art to be that the beauty it produces is the
symbol of the morally good.[109]

The imagination, as has been said, is not an ultimate faculty; it derives its importance from its connection with understanding and reason, powers which
are ultimate, the one relative to nature and the other

to freedom. Beauty, unlike the pleasant, concerns only rational animals—"not merely *quâ* rational (e.g. spirits) , but *quâ* animal also." The good, on the other hand, concerns man as purely rational. Thus Kant conceives humanity, in the first place, as an intelligent spirit; and he conceives intelligence not as essentially contemplative (there is no intellectual intuition) , but as moral (an unconditioned principle determining the will to the idea of the morally good) . The morally good is the final or absolute measure of the existence of man as a human person;[110] and hence beauty in its ultimate import is said to be the symbol of the morally good. That is the reason we speak of aesthetic duty, for every man as a moral being ought to respond to art, on pain of being judged deficient in humanity. For in art as in morality human nature is liberated from the bondage of sense and looks to the intelligible.

The relation of beauty to the morally good is merely analogical and indirect. Beauty and morality have a common source in reason as the spring of human purposes. But there are differences between them as well as analogies, so that they remain quite distinct. Beauty is not the symbol of morality because in art the will is rationally determined by the idea of good; in art the moral faculty is quiescent, implicit only. Beauty has this status because art is free of all interest, including moral interest. That is why beauty is said to be the *symbol* of the morally good. Though beauty marks a transition from nature (sense) to freedom (morality) , it is in itself autotelic.

So much for the a priori character of art, its universality and necessity. Art offers a disinterested delight which is valuable because it is a symbol of the morally good—that is, art is a mode of cognition or feeling in which we realize our humanity. Art has also an empirical and psychological side—social and historical. The empirical and the philosophic sides of art are distinct, and their connection is indirect.[111] The empirical interest cannot explain the universal import of art or the obligation we are under as human beings of cultivating the aesthetic side of our humanity. That historically people have cultivated art is an interesting empirical fact, but it does not explain that in doing so they were cultivating their humanity. From the purely empirical point of view, the past and the present have no common basis; they are external to each other, as the condition and consequent of a causal series. Empiricism conceives human experience after the pattern of physical causation. But human experience is organic; cause and effect, means and end, are not, as in a causal series, irreversible.[112] If that were the case—and so empiricism conceives it—ideas could have no effect on human behavior, and we could not distinguish between natural purposes and the purposes distinctive of humanity.

Empirically, it is nothing to us that people in the past enjoyed art. We are not they. Our needs and interests are relative to the external conditions of our own time. And since every man is the judge of his private interests and well-being, he has no cause to give up what contents him to take up what has contented others. If, however, we introduce the idea of humanity, we see the empirical facts in another light. Now past and present have a common basis. As before, the man who is indifferent to art is free to do as he wishes. It is a question of the simple, uncultivated dignity of human nature,[113] and of the right of man to be treated as an end, not as a means, whatever the level of his activity. For men, being in part autonomous beings, are free and equal, though they differ in the measure in which they realize their humanity. And in the idea of humanity we have an intellectual justification of the value we attach to distinctly human purposes, a justification, moreover, which guards the worth of simple human nature and holds out hope of liberation from the limitations of a life determined by empirical causation.

Though the empirical and philosophic aspects of art are distinct, they are indirectly related. The empirical side is based on practical interest, whereas the delight in beauty is disinterested. Yet the empirical interest in art may lay the basis for what pleases apart from all practical interest. The connection is effected by the social spirit of humanity. This spirit consists in sympathy and in the capacity for communicating feeling. We are sociable in the sense that we express our feelings and take an interest in the feelings of others. And in the light of this property of humanity, we cannot, says Kant, "escape from regarding taste as a faculty for judging everything in respect of which we can communicate our *feeling* to all other men."[114]

The social spirit, as a property of humanity, may be regarded formally, apart from specific content. It is the inclination to share our experiences, whatever their nature. And as our experiences are of two kinds, empirical and distinctly human, taste is concerned with

both. Taste, as a social property, operates as a judge
of the gratification of sense and emotion. Further, it
is a mark of civilized life, of refinement, to share the
pleasures we take in things, and indeed we come to
value pleasures according as they may be shared. We
must acknowledge, I take Kant as saying, that the con-
noisseur of wine has taste, though of a crude, empirical, kind. But the social character of taste based on
interest may lead to pure taste.

The point is well illustrated by lovers, who stand at
the apex of sociability. With lovers, it is not so much
the object of pleasure that matters as the sharing of
the pleasure. The social value is in the sharing, and
the motive of the sharing is the gratification of sense
and emotion. But this may lead to something higher.
A woman in love with a man who enjoys art may be
led to take an interest in art, and hence to enjoy
beauty, which is free of all interest, and thus to realize
this side of her humanity. And this sharing in what is
universal serves as a means of promoting the natural
inclination for society, now transformed by humanity.[115]

But people also take up art for reasons of vanity,
snobbery, gain, and the like.[116] These, too, are social
reasons, untransformed by humanity. What Kant regards as the empirical interest in art evidently varies
with the character and circumstances of people. At best
it offers a very uncertain transition from nature to freedom. Apart from the cultivation of the universal, we
get a material civilization deficient in humanity. Such
a civilization, compared with the unsophisticated state
of poor Tom, owing nothing to the worm, the beast,

the sheep, the cat, and preoccupied with the fiend and killing vermin, Kant calls a life of "splendid misery."[117]

The liberal arts, divorced from the idea of humanity, do not in practice commonly liberate—and, indeed, are not even intelligible. Art furthers the sense of humanity, and the sense of humanity promotes the enjoyment of art. The propaedeutic to art, Kant says,

> seems to lie, not in precepts, but in the culture of the mental powers by means of those elements of knowledge called *humaniora*, probably because *humanity* on the one side indicates the universal *feeling of sympathy*, and on the other the faculty of being able to *communicate* universally our inmost [feelings]. For these properties, taken together, constitute the characteristic social spirit of humanity by which it is distinguished from the limitations of animal life.[118]

The humanities are intrinsically social; they are social studies; and what are nowadays called social studies, being based on empirical causation, are not humanities.

There are critics today who tell us that literary scholarship—history—is a branch of sociology; and there are historians who have come to regard history as sociology. But a discipline is defined not merely by its subject matter, but more especially by its point of view. The reduction of the humanities to the social sciences is the consequence of a confusion between two distinct points of view. The object of humane studies is not man regarded as an object implicated in physical causation; it is, in general, history—that is, the synthesis of nature and freedom—the second nature,

Kant calls it—created by the transformation of the given by the autonomy of the human spirit. Art itself is a synthesis, a specialized form of "history." Art and the morally good have a common source in reason. So far as art involves the given, it is not fully intelligible in abstraction from history, though the ultimate import of art cannot be derived from empirical fact alone.[119]

If the humanities are intrinsically social, the reason is that the "intelligible substrate" of life is the presupposition of human society. That is the starting point; and beyond that, according to Kant, we cannot go in our efforts to render history intelligible; for the rest we must look to experience. Man is man in virtue of his capacity for thought and feeling, and also in virtue of his capacity for, and interest in, the expression of thought and feeling. The working out of human destiny—the development of man's humanity—is a historical process, effected through social life. It is man's moral nature—freedom and ideas of reason—that creates a rational society—a society of laws and of established procedures for the communication of thought and feeling.[120] Kant thinks of moral feeling and cognition—the practical and theoretical aspects of man—as natural and original powers, and of taste, regarded as a critical faculty operative in the members of a society, as a development presupposing moral feeling and cognition.[121] In short, the existence of pure taste, as a social property of humanity, presupposes a certain degree of intellectual and moral culture.[122] And this is brought about by the social spirit of humanity, working as the communication of thought and feeling. Once this stage has been reached, art may be a humanizing influence, by evoking the feeling of liberated humanity. Thus social progress promotes art, and art promotes social progress, conceived as the realization of humanity.

Kant's argument in behalf of pure aesthetic taste is that, since knowledge is possible—Kant is not a skeptic —the aesthetic attitude is possible, for both presuppose the same subjective conditions. In order to illustrate what he means by taste as a *sensus communis,* he compares it with understanding as a sense common to everyone. The maxims of "common human understanding" are:

(1) to think for oneself; (2) to put ourselves in thought in the place of everyone else; (3) always to think consistently. The first is the maxim of *unprejudiced* thought; the second of *enlarged* thought; the third of *consecutive* thought.[123]

Everyone, in virtue of his humanity, Kant presumes, is capable of thinking critically, impartially, and consistently. Critical thought frees one from prejudice and superstition, and thus makes for enlightenment. In the narrower sense, enlightenment is not moral behavior, but skepticism—not Pyrrhonism, but the negative capacity for suspending judgment and for examining things critically, for oneself. This, Kant thinks, is very difficult to maintain or restore, especially in the public mind.

Of the three maxims, the second is the most germane to taste,[124] and to the mental culture which is the object of humane studies—enlargement of mind. The first maxim has to do with understanding, the third with reason, and the second with judgment. It is "reflective judgment and not sensation" which is the standard of art as beauty.[125] Both the aesthetic and the intellectual judgment involve the "operation of reflection," which frees one from the limitations of "the subjective private conditions of his own judgment."[126] By taking thought we escape the illusion that judgments based on private conditions have objective validity. Taking thought means imaginative sympathy and the comparison of one's judgment with the "collective reason of humanity." In this way we attain to a *universal standpoint.* The enlargement of mind Kant speaks of, so far as it is a product of the social spirit of mankind, includes learning—the best ideas, of the past as well as of the present. But what Kant has in mind more particularly is the philosophic habit of mind: the "generality of outlook"[127] which corrects the private bias of the ego and which, by adjusting behavior to intellectual insight, transforms the egoistic sensibility into a liberal or humane personality.

The direct social value of art is that it is a mode of communicating feeling apart from the mediation of concepts. It is thus differentiated from representations communicating thought, determinate concepts and ideas of reason. Still, indirectly art is an instrument for the cultivation of the mental powers. It produces a wealth of indeterminate thought and thus provides an abundance of material for reflection. The use the mind makes of this material is not objective, but subjective. Art stirs the mind, strengthens it, and enlarges it—by elevating it to the contemplation of aesthetic ideas. The cultural value of art arises from the complexity of references, for the whole man is involved in art.[128]

Thus far Kant has been speaking of the cultural value of art of the first rank, of art as the production of (free) beauty. There is also "dependent" art and beauty—art determined by concepts and producing concepts. If (as Eliot does) we extend the term "imitation" to cover the presentation of aesthetic ideas, we may speak of art of the first rank as mimetic and of art of the second as didactic; or, as Kant does, in one passage,[129] we may differentiate between aesthetics and art—art as the adjustment of means to ends, art which presents a theme or thesis.

Kant's first concern is to distinguish beauty from the pleasant and the good. That difference acknowledged, he is quite ready to affirm the cultural value of didactic art. He thus preserves, though in a subordinate status, the Platonic, Roman, and Renaissance view of the moral value of art. Didactic art is a civilizing influence, in respect to society as well as to the individual. Art may, with profit to the whole man, be combined with the good. The good has a practical side, desire, and an intellectual side, reason. The good as perfection involves the reference of form to the concept of an object. That is an intellectual, though noncognitive, judgment; at the same time, it involves the satisfaction of moral feeling—the sense that things are as reason would have them. Art, then, as differentiated from aesthetics, unlike theoretical judgment, combines sensibility with intellect, the whole person gaining thereby. Still, beauty, which is self-subsistent, and perfection, which depends on concepts, are quite distinct; and neither considered in itself gains by combination with the other.[130] And Kant is concerned, in the first place, with the elucidation of beauty and with its intellectual justification as an experience which is universal and necessary.

Kant wrote his *Critique* before his countrymen formulated the systematic theory of historical scholarship. Still, he offers a few remarks on this head. Since there is no "science of the beautiful, but only a critique of it," it is a mistake to speak of "historical sciences" as "beautiful sciences" (belles lettres?). The source of the confusion, he says,

> is without doubt nothing else than this, as it has been rightly remarked, that for beautiful art in its entire completeness much science is requisite, e.g. a knowledge of ancient languages, a learned familiarity with classical authors, history, a knowledge of antiquities, etc. And hence these historical sciences, because they form the necessary preparation and basis for beautiful art, and also partly because under them is included the knowledge of the products of beautiful art (rhetoric and poetry), have come to be called beautiful sciences by a transposition of words.[131]

Kant's philosophy is critical. It does not teach a system of beliefs. It is concerned rather with the analysis of the presuppositions—the a priori conditions—of experience. It analyzes the sources and limitations of the various types of experience. Its proper use is negative; it purges rather than extends our knowledge;[132] it rectifies and clarifies thought. The general effect of Kant's work is to clarify thought without impoverishing it. Further, he restates the humanism of

Greek philosophy in the light of scholastic logic, the experimental science of the seventeenth century, and the humanitarian feeling of the eighteenth. As for his aesthetics, it is a great pity that it is written in such a trying style. Nevertheless, this dry, technical analysis of art and beauty is the modern counterpart of Aristotle's analysis of mimetic poetry. The influence of both works has, on the whole, been indirect; for Kant comes to us through adapters whose relation to the *Critique* is analogous to that of Renaissance commentators to the *Poetics*. These two books are the seed-beds of literary theory.

ELIOT IS, UP TO a point, an aesthetic critic. And as
for general aesthetics, it begins properly with Kant.
Moreover, it may be said that subsequent writers on
the subject—Hegel and Croce, to name but two—have
in the main restated Kant's notions in terms of their
respective philosophies.[133]

Eliot's formula for poetry, quoted in the passage
dealing with Coleridge and Shakespeare—"thinking-
in-images"—exactly expresses, I believe, the Kantian
resolution of the paradox of art and beauty. Again, at
a venture, I should say that his essay "The Social
Function of Poetry" is Kantian, though it exhibits
the subtlety of adapation and application we find everywhere in his work. Here is one passage.

We may say that the duty of the poet, as poet, is only indirectly to his people: his direct duty is to his *language,* first to preserve, and second to extend and improve. In expressing what other people feel he is also changing the feeling by making it more conscious; he is making people more aware of what they feel already, and therefore teaching them something about themselves. But he is not merely a more conscious person than the others; he is also individually different from other people, and from other poets too, and can make his readers share consciously in new feelings which they had not experienced before. That is the difference between the writer who is merely eccentric or mad and the genuine poet. The former may have feelings which are unique but which cannot be shared, and are therefore useless; the latter discovers new variations of sensibility which can be appropriated by others. And in expressing them he is developing and enriching the language which he speaks.[134]

In this essay, in order to make clear what he does not mean by the social function of poetry, he distinguishes between the function of didactic poetry—poetry which has "a deliberate, conscious social purpose"— and the function of "poetry as poetry." "Poetry," he says, "has primarily to do with the expression of feeling and emotion." "And this is what I mean by the social function of poetry in its largest sense: that it does, in proportion to its excellence and vigour affect the speech and the sensibility of the whole nation."[135]

That Eliot is an aesthetic critic is written on every page of his criticism. It is this that gives his critical output its coherence. The "problem of the integrity of poetry" is an aesthetic problem, and the consideration of poetry "primarily as poetry and not another thing" is a statement of the aesthetic point of view. And Eliot has held to this point of view, as far as it goes, throughout his work, early and late.

This position accounts partly for the negations and disclaimers which characterize his writing. Poetry, he says, is "a superior amusement," though that of course is not a "true definition."[136] But then no single definition will do. Certainly poetry is not morals or religion, and yet poetry certainly has something to do with these activities—"though we cannot say what." Further, the development of poetry is not independent of social change, though social change alone cannot explain poetry.[137] So critical theory is and is not helpful; if a poem is moving, it means something, though what it means will depend on theory. As to the use of poetry, people claim too little or too much. It is best to assume that we do not know what poetry is or does or ought to do, nor should we suppose that we have any clear notion of what "use" is.[138]

In "The Function of Criticism," Eliot says: "I have assumed as axiomatic that a creation, a work of art, is autotelic; and that criticism, by definition, is *about* something other than itself." Again : "I do not deny that art may be affirmed to serve ends beyond itself; but art is not required to be aware of these ends, and indeed performs its function, whatever that may be, according to various theories of value, much better by indifference to them."[139]

Besides aesthetics, there are theories of value. Aesthetics is, in a sense, a negative position. It says what poetry is not, but it does not say what it is or does or ought to do. In short, there are as many aesthetic theories as there are philosophies.

In "The Frontiers of Criticism," Eliot says: "I have been somewhat bewildered to find, from time to time, that I am regarded as one of the ancestors of modern criticism, if too old to be a modern critic myself."[140] If Eliot's relation to modern criticism has been misconstrued, the reason is that due weight has not been given to the influence of his extra-literary views on his criticism. Eliot and I. A. Richards are both aesthetic critics, but they hold different theories of value and of knowledge; they agree on what poetry is not, but they disagree on what it is and what it is for.

Few critics with Eliot's qualifications have gone so far as he in trying to isolate "the essentially poetic," and his conclusion is that "we bring our pursuit in the end to something insignificant."[141] He means, I think, that, if we isolate "the essentially poetic" from everything else that concerns us, we are left with a vacuity. Aesthetics is not a pure, but a mixed, study. There is no point, Eliot says, at which the criticism of poetry stops and other domains begin. "The greatness of literature," he says, "cannot be determined solely by literary standards; though we must remember that whether it is literature or not can be determined only by literary standards."[142]

This position, it seems to me, follows from his philosophic and religious views. His philosophic notions are in the metaphysical tradition of the Greeks (the tradition of Aristotle rather than Plato). That tradition includes the scholastic thinkers of the Middle Ages. For Eliot, it also includes Bradley; for what Eliot values in Bradley is not his Hegelian, but his

Greek, connections[143]—though Hegel, as Bradley points out, is also indebted to the Greeks.

Though a student of philosophy, Eliot is not, according to his lights, a philosopher—that is not his profession. His métier is that of poet and critic. More generally, he is a man of letters, and an apologist for religion. He has ideas of various kinds, and these show everywhere in his work, where they are assimilated to the purpose in hand. But in his view poetry is concerned not with ideas, but with emotion; and emotion, with him, is the equivalent of thought. As a poet, he is concerned, on the whole, with the unspecified religious consciousness, as, for example, in *The Waste Land*, where he draws on various religious traditions in order to generalize the "theme" of spiritual sterility. His poetry is religious poetry, not because it treats of obvious religious subjects, but because it views life in a religious perspective,[144] though without explicitly evoking the criteria of religion. Everything depends on the tone, the attitude, the implication, and the ultimate intention.

He has said that in literature it is not belief that matters, but assent.[145] Belief is a question of psychological attitude, whereas assent is a matter of understanding. Still, belief has a formal side; for it varies according to its object, philosophic belief differing from scientific as well as from poetic assent. Again, philosophy is not psychology, though psychology is a part of philosophy; nor is it the understanding required for poetic assent. Philosophy is a matter of intellectual truth, which is different from the satisfaction or frustration of desire, though it satisfies in part the desire for truth. It differs, too, from understanding, which is a state of mind comprising more than learning and less than intellectual judgment. Understanding, it would appear, has to do with the apprehension of the possibilities of human experience and with the attitudes and beliefs to which experience gives rise; it is virtually one with wisdom, the grasp of human values. Further, philosophy, though competent within its limits, affords an imperfect knowledge of things. Without wisdom it is vain; and it has no direct knowledge of supersensible reality. Philosophy is completed by theology, which, employing philosophy in a secondary office, rests on the authority of the Bible. Finally, theology itself is transcended in mystic vision.

This is the spirit and method of metaphysical thought, the mode of thought of Aristotle, the scholastics, and Bradley. Its character is owing partly to the logic of identity and partly to the practice of starting with what is given in experience. Everything that exists is something in itself, individual and specific, so that the world is conceived as an order of irreducible substances, activities, and qualities. Nothing, as Eliot has it, is "a substitute for anything else."[146]

In speaking of the scholastic element in Eliot's thought, I refer to the version renovated and refurbished by its modern exponents, say, about the turn of the present century. It is a scholasticism not of the thirteenth, but of the twentieth, century—a new scholasticism. It discriminates between what it considers to be essential in the medieval version and what merely accessory. It disengages a nucleus of certain broad psychological and metaphysical principles which it applies to the data of modern experience. It draws on whatever aspects of modern thought—philosophic, scientific, historical—might serve to improve its views. Its general object is to take up new positions without abandoning the old ones, to blend tradition and innovation. Like its medieval predecessor, it is "a specific eclecticism." Its aim is to bring the scholastic point of view into touch with the modern mind and to adapt itself, within limits, to the needs and conditions of modern life. It is presented as an autonomous philosophic discipline, the broad principles of which, now as in the Middle Ages, are capable of diverse interpretation. Its first concern is to defend the validity of the metaphysics of Aristotle against the views of modern idealism and positivism. Finally, it is offered as independent of any particular religion. In natural religion, its first concern is to establish the reality of the religious consciousness itself as exhibited in the history of mankind.[147]

Though the scholastic element in Eliot's thought is of the first importance, it does not bulk nearly so large as the Bradleyan element. Indeed, it would be hard to exaggerate Eliot's debt to Bradley. Eliot's assimilation of Bradley has been so thorough that it nourishes every part of his work. It is possible, of course, to have a general understanding of Eliot's work apart from Bradley, but for a particular understanding we must know something about Bradley. And the problem is that Bradley, in his way, is no less difficult and complex than Eliot.

CHAPTER 5

F. H. BRADLEY

THE PLACE THAT EMOTION occupies in Eliot's theory of poetry is due not to scholasticism, or to Kant, but to Bradley. Bradley's theory of experience supplies, as it were, an emotional basis for scholastic logic, though it also requires a modification of that logic. In Bradley's view, the older logic is valid only in the sphere of abstraction, where the pure intellect is engaged. It does not serve for the analysis of experience as Bradley conceives of it.[148]

Bradley begins with experience conceived as a whole of feeling in which thought and volition are implicit; and he identifies this form with reality, that is to say, the Absolute, together with its stages and degrees. Reality takes the form of an "individual totality" or a "concrete universal." The form is that of an organic whole. The unity of the whole is a universal, and the concreteness lies in the particular parts. Either aspect taken by itself is an abstraction. For the whole lives only in its parts, though it is something other than its parts; and the parts live only in the whole, in which they find their meaning and value. Further, the whole is always at bottom a whole of feeling; feeling becomes an object of thought; and yet there remains at bottom a whole of feeling—the reservoir is inexhaustible.[149] In this view, contradictions, in the ordinary sense, become merely differences: there are no divisions, only distinctions and relations within a whole of feeling. When we have a contradiction, Bradley says, in effect, we must look to feeling, and there we find the ground of connection and distinction—unity and diversity.[150] This, in outline, is the character of experience and reality, the object of philosophic analysis.

The general result, I should say, is a complication of the older mode of thought. There is, to begin with, a more detailed dialectic of feeling than in Greek or scholastic thought; indeed, in one sense, it is all a dialectic feeling. As a consequence, the distinctions and qualifications are complex and shifting. The complication is especially telling in the relation of thought and feeling. Thought and feeling are not mutually exclusive; they are merely different: related and distinct, and at bottom one. Each participates, to a certain extent, in the other; and, as it does, each is transformed, and yet it does not altogether lose its former character. For example, when thought is taken up into a whole of feeling (as in a poem), it is no longer thought; it ceases to be merely ideal, an abstraction, and takes on reality. Again, when feeling is transformed into thought, it is no longer pure feeling, that is, no longer, as Bradley has it, immediate; it has become an object of thought, an idea, touched with ideality. Hence feeling as such can never be described, for to think of it is to transform it. Feeling can be felt, but it can be known only by its objectification in thought, action, and art. In art, the object of our perception is feeling. As we shall see, feeling, when objectified, loses its particularity and becomes universal. Feelings, as objects of perception, are universals. The general difference, it may be said, between feeling and thought is that one is implicit and the other explicit. And understanding comprises both forms, intuitive and discursive. It is this aspect of Bradley's philosophy that perhaps more than any other shows itself in Eliot's criticism. Eliot, on one occasion, goes so far as to describe some lines of Donne's as "hovering" between thought and feeling.

Eliot's view of the economy of mind is based largely on Bradley, though subject to what may be called scholastic reservations. For instance, the note on poetry and belief appended to the essay on Dante is clearly an adaptation of Bradley. It is the parallel of the argument which Bradley makes most explicitly in connection with philosophy.[151] Poetry, like philosophy, so the argument goes, is a special activity, subject to special conditions. The principles which regulate it are, within the limits of aesthetics, absolute. If one denies this, one denies the existence of poetry, and hence of responsible criticism. In short, if one chooses to discuss poetry, or philosophy, one must be prepared to observe the rules of the game.

Eliot, especially when discussing the relation of poetry and philosophy, reflects as a rule Bradley's view of the place of intellect in life, a view somewhat different from that of scholasticism. With scholasticism, reason, though it has its limits, is within those limits supreme—the rule of life. Apart from it, there is no morality, or, for that matter, art. With Bradley, the intellect plays a more specialized role in life. The intellect, with Bradley, is, to be sure, entangled with the rest of life, but it is something less than the rule of life.[152] The intellect offers but the satisfaction of a special impulse, the desire to satisfy the mind and the mind only. The other desires of life must look for satisfaction to the special functions relative to them. Further, the satisfaction of the intellect is not only different from other satisfactions, but, from one point of view, is neither superior nor inferior to them.

The sole concern of the intellect is with theory, and within theory the rule of the intellect is absolute. Moreover, theory is not feeling.[153] It is feeling, not theory, that is the ground of the views of life, the attitudes and outlooks, which popularly pass for philosophy. Nor is theory in its essence practical; for neither the utility nor the goodness of an idea is a guarantee of its intellectual truth. The fact that our working ideas satisfy our impulses and desires does not make them intellectually valid; and to suppose that it does is the ruin of philosophy as an intellectual discipline. Outside theory, however, the intellect has no title to dictate to morality or religion, so that these are independent of theoretical criteria. These last, on the other hand, have no jurisdiction over intellect in

what concerns theory and knowledge or over art in
what concerns beauty.

Morality is concerned with the good, the satisfaction and harmony of all sides of life. Accordingly, as
coextensive with life, morality has something to say
about the bounds within which philosophy and art
may be pursued. But this being an external regulation, it does not touch the specific principle of these
activities. Philosophy and art, when engaged in their
own business, are independent of the practical side of
life—though in the larger sense, as satisfying human
desires, they are both practical. Indeed, it is the moral
duty of the artist, as of the inquirer, within the limits
of his art, to pursue his art independently of external
rule; for in that way he serves best the good of the
whole—supposing, as Bradley does, that man's nature
is a unity.

But art and science are not in themselves social
virtues; their social bearing is indirect. Neither artist
nor inquirer is obligated to consider ends falling outside art and science, each of which finds its justification
in its own end. Nor is there any necessary connection,
Bradley thinks, between art and science, on the one
hand, and, on the other, social life. The content—
the perceptions and emotions—of art and science is
different from that of social life. It is only on the supposition that physical existence is the ultimate end
of society that art and science can be held to be essentially means to social ends. And such a supposition,
Bradley holds, is in direct conflict with the facts of
moral consciousness. The end of society, on a secular
level, is the realization of the moral ideal, the content
of which is both social and cultural. And though Brad-

ley does not impugn the importance of social life, he holds that art and science constitute the higher part of that ideal. It is our moral duty to perfect our nature by the cultivation of art and science, not merely as means to social ends, but as ends in themselves.[154]

Bradley, like Plato and Aristotle, like Kant and Hegel, is concerned with finding an intellectual justification of the values which give human life its meaning and worth. To Bradley, English utilitarianism and American pragmatism (and by implication, at least, French positivism) offer no support for the order of values which traditionally has defined the meaning of civilization. Bradley's refutation of the philosophy based on the method and outlook of the physical sciences is directed at the nominalism underlying its psychology and logic, and at the ethics based on these studies. Its ethics, he thinks, is at variance with the facts of the moral consciousness; indeed, to him, it does not represent a moral concept at all. The difference in ethical views may be expressed by saying that for Bradley and the tradition he represents self-expression is not self-realization.

The utilitarian doctrine of individualism holds that only particulars are real and that particulars sustain only external relations to one another. Thus the self is merely a collection of particulars, of sensations or feelings, the aggregate held together by memory or principles of association. In this view, the self is a sum of a series of events in time and space. This sum, regarded as exclusive of other sums, is what is meant by an individual; and only such individuals are real. The individual, so conceived, is, once more, a sum of feelings and desires; and his actions, verbal and non-verbal, represent the self-expression of his individuality. But the individual, in this view, is a bare existence, an atomic unit, with no reference beyond itself. It is merely subjective, existing as moments of transient feelings devoid of import; beyond the fact of feeling, as pleasure and pain, its existence signifies nothing.

Self-realization, with Bradley, involves the relation of the private self to what he denominates the ideal self or the universal will. It is by the realization of values represented by such a will, values independent of the self in the sense of being objective and not merely subjective, that the private self finds its meaning and worth. In other words, the private self takes on meaning only by its relation to self-transcendent contexts—moral, intellectual, aesthetic, and religious. In short, the significance attributed to human life presupposes the existence of a metaphysical universe. Apart from such a universe, there is self-expression, but no self-realization.

Bradley's objection to the utilitarian doctrine is, first, that it is dogmatic—assumed, not proved. Secondly, it fails to account for the facts of morality, philosophy, art, and religion, all of which, as Bradley says, exist. In effect, it leaves the part of human experience which is regarded as something other than events in time and space unintelligible, without rational explanation or justification.

The empirical self, Bradley observes, is the subject matter of the sciences of phenomena. To the psychologist, for instance, mental facts are merely a kind of occurrence in time and space. But psychology is not logic or ethics or metaphysics. It has, properly speaking, nothing to say about reality and value. Psychologists, however, owing to a narrow culture imparted by a bad education, tend to mistake themselves for philosophers. They misconstrue the working ideas they employ to direct and organize their study for first principles treating of the ultimate nature of things. One may, if one chooses, ignore all aspects of experience which fall outside the sphere of the sciences of phenomena; but ignorance of the rest of life does not make a philosopher. One may, if one chooses, think so, and dispense with philosophy; but psychology and philosophy can never be reduced one to the other.[156]

With Bradley, the moral point of view is not final; moral experience, social and cultural, does not exhaust the content of human life. The realization of the moral ideal remains ever incomplete; and this moral imperfection implies a stage of unity higher than and beyond the aspiration of morality. The imperfection of moral life leads to "the necessity of a religious point of view."[157]

Religion is essentially a higher form of goodness than morality. Hence there are points in which the two are alike and points in which they differ. The psychological form of both is the same; for the will— not mere feeling or theory—is of the essence of both. Religion, like morality, is essentially practical; and when it ceases to be practical, it ceases to be religion. Therefore all moral duties, social and cultural, are also religious duties, though morality is not religion. The difference is that the object of religion, the supreme good, has a different status from the object of morality. In general, the good we seek to realize is an ideal self which is other than our private selves (or it is a will, a good will, a universal will, which is different from our private wills) . In morality, the ideal self is a mere ideal: it is something which is to be, but is not yet, and never really is. In religion, this ideal is real; it is a "real ideal"; it is "all and the whole reality." This difference in the status of the object accounts for the difference in the content of morality and religion. Thus for morality, in spite of the sense of discrepancy between the ideal and its realization, the self and the world are viewed as real. For religion, however, to be alienated from divine will is sin; and that means that the self and the world are felt and known as what is not, as unreal.[158]

So much for the relation between morality and religion. As for art and science, they are both alike and unlike these last. Their moral aspect consists in the aim at perfection rather than self-expression. In this sense, as involving will and the aim at an ideal, they are like both morality and religion. Again, they are like religion and unlike morality in that their objects, beauty and truth, are viewed as real, not merely ideal. Finally, they are unlike both morality and religion in that what comes first in art and science is the result, and this falls outside the will.

The artist aims at beauty and the inquirer at truth; and the significance of these activities, like that of religion in respect to its object, presupposes the reality of beauty and truth. Thus in logic it is assumed that the ideal universe of concepts is real, and that implication is real. So in art it is assumed that beauty is not merely an event in the head of the artist, but is objectively real.[159] The end in art and science is that some "unseen object" should be "seen" to be realized; the end is "the sight of the object as such."[160] The end, that is to say, is contemplation. The artist or the inquirer has it in his power to make the object "to exist or to appear," but it is not in his power to make it be "that which it is."[161] We have the power to recognize beauty and truth, to realize them, but the character of these objects is independent of our wills. Though beauty and truth are objects of human need and desire, these objects in their specific nature fall outside the sphere of the will. Though practical, they are still not subordinate to practice.

The objects of art and science, then, like the object of religion, are viewed as real. Yet religion is neither art nor science, nor is it a form or mixture of the two. In the first place, there is a difference in their objects; for beauty and truth are but aspects of reality, whereas the supreme good of religion is for religion the complete reality. Again, the will is of the essence of religion, but it is only incidental to the result which is of the essence of art and science. Thirdly, the reality of the religious object is wholly dependent on faith— that is, "the belief in the reality of an object, and the will that that object be real."[162]

These activities, then, are different; but difference with Bradley signifies not division, but distinction and relation. And Bradley draws an important inference from their relation.

No doubt it would be a great mistake to forget that art and science involve will, and the will of particular persons, and that it is this will which realizes the object; and that hence, since the object of science and art is at least partly identical with the object of religion, both science and art may so far be said to imply religion, since they

imply the relation of the particular will to the real
ideal.[163]

This implication, I take it, is based on the supposition
that "the human-divine life is one process," and that
art and science and religion are "distinguishable elements or aspects of this one whole process." If this is
so, it follows that "neither art nor science nor religion
can exist as a thing by itself, and the two former will
necessarily imply the latter."[164]

A philosopher or artist, says Bradley, the moment
he "is conscious of his will in relation to the real ideal,
as a will which has demands on him, . . . ceases to be a
mere philosopher or artist as such (which after all no
human being is), and becomes also religious or irreligious"—or at least "moral."

Bradley wrote no separate work on aesthetics. His
aesthetics is implicit in his general philosophy—his
logic, ethics, and metaphysics. His explicit treatment
of this subject is general and fragmentary. It consists
of remarks made in connection with other aspects of
his philosophy, and is intelligible as a rule only in the
light of the non-aesthetic parts of his work. Thus a
large part of his explicit discussion of aesthetics occurs
in the course of a demonstration that all finite modes
of experience fall short of the Absolute.

Though a philosopher of the Absolute, Bradley is
yet a kind of dualist. But dualism with him is not the
ultimate fact about the universe; it is merely interme-
diary and transitory. All finite modes of experience
are marked by a duality of feeling and idea. Reality is

a unity of these two aspects attained by transcending this distinction. What it comes to, in effect, is this: first, we feel the world; then we both feel and think it by turns; and finally we endeavor to transcend the duality of feeling and thought in a way which comprises both and yet is neither. Though we cannot experience the ultimate reality in detail, we do experience its various appearances; and we can form a general idea of the Absolute based on the analysis of what we do experience.[165]

The all-inclusive reality is the Absolute; and the Absolute is exhibited in its appearances, which represent, more or less, a stage or degree of the ultimate reality. The form of reality, in all cases, is, more or less, a mode of being or experience which is an individual totality. Such a totality is, more or less, self-contained, independent, and unique. Again, with Bradley, two terms and a relation constitute a contradiction, that is to say, something which requires to be supplemented from the outside, which is determined by external relations—in short, something which is not self-existent, but tends to pass beyond itself into a larger unity.

As judged by these criteria, art stands above theory and practice and next to religion in the order of reality, though the ultimate reality, the Absolute, is something distinct from all these.

The aesthetic attitude is a distinct mode of experience, distinguished from theory (perception and thought), practice (will and desire), feeling, and pleasure and pain (Bradley does not identify feeling with pleasure and pain). Yet most if not all of these modes of experience are components of the aesthetic attitude, so that art next to religion comes closest to manifesting the all-inclusive reality. "In the aesthetic attitude we may seem at last to have transcended the opposition of idea to existence, and to have at last surmounted and risen beyond the relational consciousness." And the reason is that in art we *seem* to have a concrete whole of feeling and also a self-contained object in which fact and meaning are one. And "this aspect of the world satisfies us in a way unattainable by theory or practice, and it plainly cannot be reduced and resolved into either."[166]

In a work of art we have a "felt whole, as felt," or, what is the same thing, "a non-relational unity."[167] The experience of art is a unity of feeling lying below the level of discursive thought. Our tendency in art is to rest content in the enjoyment of the work *as though* it were a self-contained object, having no reference beyond itself and undetermined by anything external to it. This is the "aesthetic attitude," which Bradley defines in general as "the self-existent emotional."[168] The experience of art is a state of feeling, a feeling of unity in diversity; and this state of feeling stands by itself, self-contained and independent, a specialized form of reality.

The moment we begin to reflect and to analyze, the unity of the aesthetic attitude is dissolved into the dichotomy of feeling and thought.[169] Our activity ceases to be aesthetic and becomes intellectual. On one side is the experience we have had, on the other the object which occasioned it. We can make either one of these sides or both the object of analysis, with the aim of determining the character of the content— its qualities and relations. And this undertaking is a new and distinct activity. Furthermore, in reflecting upon the work, we seek to explain and understand it not only in itself, but also as an object determined by external conditions and causes. In all this—our concern with the experience itself and with historical exegesis—our aim is not aesthetic, but intellectual, satisfaction. We endeavor to reconstruct the aesthetic state, not in fact, but in thought, ideally.

Bradley defines beauty as "the self-existent pleasant."[170] As I take it, this means, for one thing, that beauty is not self-enjoyment; it is not the self enjoying itself; feeling in this sense, self-feeling, is not beauty. Nor, again, is beauty an idea or set of ideas; for ideas, being abstractions, are not self-existent. Beauty is, on one side, an object which is independent of the self, and, on the other, a whole of feeling, and, again, it involves the relation between these two sides.

Beauty, accordingly, cannot stand by itself, for it is a union of inconsistent characters. In the first place, pleasure is of the essence of beauty, and pleasure must be the pleasure of someone, so that beauty is determined by something outside itself, a quality in the person who enjoys it. Further, since beauty is an object of perception, it is determined by the relation involved in perception. Hence "both as perceived and as emotional" beauty is determined by external causes.[171]

If we consider beauty apart from the self, and suppose that the beautiful exists independently, we arrive at the same result. Beauty so regarded is composed of two elements, expression and content. A poem, say, is made up of language and meaning. These two aspects, though they may appear to be inseparable, are in fact never so. The language may be an imperfect expression of the content, or the content may be too broad or too narrow for its expression. For instance, since language is symbolic, the elements of expression, words and images, tend to lose their particularity and to turn into universals, so that we entertain the idea in separation from its expression, entertain something merely ideal, an abstraction.[172] Again, a poem, after all, does not write itself. Its expression is conditioned by external causes, biographical and historical. Thus the various aspects of the aesthetic object tend to fall apart.

Religion stands higher than art and beauty in the order of reality, at least in the sense that for religion its object is the complete reality; but it, too, is something less than the Absolute, the ultimate reality.

Religion takes diverse forms, higher and lower, complete and incomplete. Religion in general is "a fixed feeling of fear, resignation, admiration or approval, no matter what may be the object, provided only that this feeling reaches a certain strength, and is qualified by a certain degree of reflection." "Hence any object, in regard to which we feel a supreme fear or approval, will engage our devotion, and be for us a Deity. And this object, most emphatically, in no other sense need possess divinity."[173] In this general sense religion varies with the object of devotion—a woman, a pursuit, and the like. But these are incomplete forms. Religion in the highest sense is "devotion to the one perfect object which is utterly good." It is this form of religion with which Bradley is concerned, and, in particular, with the modern Christian consciousness.

The essence of religion, as has been noted, is practical. It consists in the relation of the will of the self to the supreme will; and its object is the realization of perfect goodness. These are the basic elements of a structure which is accepted by many as ordering and harmonizing every aspect of life. Yet as judged by the theoretical criteria Bradley employs, the structure is fundamentally inconsistent.[174]

The contradictions of religion are part of its very nature; for religion involves two terms and a relation, and that, as has been observed, is the very form of contradiction. Moreover, in Bradley's view, the contradictions cannot be removed without destroying religion as that has come to be understood. And Bradley's conclusion is that contradiction is inseparable from religion.

I need but give a sampling here of the many variations Bradley plays on this theme. The essence of religion lies in the relation of the self to God. Both the self and God are viewed as independently real; yet in religion the self apart from God and God apart from the self are abstractions devoid of meaning. Hence the self and God are both independently real and mutually dependent. Again, if independently real, the relation between the two must be external; yet the heart of religion is the experience of God as a presence within the self. Thus God is both external to and immanent in the self. Or take the other aspect of religion. If the self realizes the perfect good, the self is no longer the self it was, with its experience of harmony and discord in respect to God, so that the relation which

defines religion is abolished; and with this termina-
tion religion ceases to be religion and is transformed
into something else.[175]

Bradley's point is that these various aspects are all
essential to the religious consciousness, that they cannot be disjoined without religion's suffering a fatal
deterioration, and that they are thoroughly incon-
sisent.

> The religious consciousness rests on the felt unity of
> unreduced opposites: and either to combine these con-
> sistently, or upon the other hand to transform them is
> impossible for religion. And hence self-contradiction in
> theory, and oscillation in sentiment, is inseparable from
> its essence. Its dogmas must end in one-sided error, or
> else in senseless compromise.[176]

Is all, then, lost? Does this spell ruin for religion?
No, says Bradley, not if we modify our claims, not if
we separate the essential from the incidental in religion. For one thing, religion, from the theoretical
point of view, is in the same case as every other mode
of finite experience: all are contradictory and hence
something less than ultimate truth. Then theoretical
consistency is perhaps unattainable anywhere; and, in
any event, it is not to be found in life and practice or
in the special sciences. In these spheres, untroubled
by the lack of theoretical consistency, we manage to
get along with partial truths and inconsistent ideas
so long as they seem to serve our various purposes.

After all, the essence of religion is neither theory
nor feeling; the essence is practical, and the central
point is faith. Further, historically, religion has flour-

ished independently of any particular doctrine or cult. Doctrine and cult, though involved in religion, are not of its essence. The essence of religion is not the holding of orthodox views, or the aesthetic excitements of cult, or the ministrations of clergymen. From the point of view of religion, these are not ends, but means. Of course religion must have its doctrine; it must have ideas which give expression to its needs and satisfactions. But the criterion of religious ideas is not theoretic; it is practical. Those ideas and practices are true and right that serve the end of religion, which is the realization of the perfect good. Thus the ideas of religion are working ideas. And in this respect they are like the ideas of all other special disciplines; they represent not ultimate, but special, truths; and it is a mistake to judge them by standards external to religion.[177]

Though Bradley does not pretend to know, or to know how one goes about deciding, what ideas and practices are true and right for religion, he has some notions about what is essential and what incidental to religion. In his view, the chief religious truth is the idea of the "real presence" of God within the self. This truth must not be denied or impaired; and all other truths must be formulated in such a way as to agree with and support this primary truth.[178]

Consider, for example, the idea of a personal God. For Bradley, the only important sense of personality is that of a "finite and mutable" self. The idea of God, then, as a person and as infinite is inconsistent. But this is a secondary matter so long as the truth of the "real presence" of the "Good Will" in the self is retained. Further, if this is the central truth of religion, there is, Bradley says, no escaping some form of pantheism. And pantheism is inconsistent with the idea of an individual Creator who is external to the self and the world. Finally, personal immortality, Bradley thinks, is highly improbable; and, in his opinion, it is not, or ought not to be, necessary to morality and religion.[179]

CHAPTER 6

PHILOSOPHY AND RELIGION

THE STRUCTURE OF BRADLEY's thought is not dissimilar
to Kant's. The content, however, is different. Kant conceives the basic act of experience as knowledge, whereas
Bradley conceives it as a whole of feeling. And there is
a difference, as a consequence, in their logic. Bradley's
structure of thought is reflected everywhere in Eliot,
and his notion of experience forms the basis of Eliot's
poetics. But before proceeding to these matters, I wish
to consider Eliot's attitude towards Bradley's view of
religion.

Eliot, in his essay on Bradley, says that "it is easy to
underestimate Hegel, but it is easy to overestimate
Bradley's debt to Hegel; in a philosophy like Bradley's the points at which he *stops* are always important
points."

Where exactly does Bradley stop? Perhaps the presence of Hegel in this passage suggests that Bradley, unlike Hegel, does not view philosophy as the completion of religion. At any rate, what Bradley says of religion varies somewhat with the context. In *Ethical Studies,* he says: "We purpose to say nothing about the ultimate truth of religion: nothing again about its origin in the world, or in the individual. We are to take the religious consciousness as an existing fact, and to take it as we find it now in the modern Christian mind, whether that mind recognizes it or whether it does not."[180] In *Appearance and Reality* and *Essays on Truth and Reality,* he does say things which bear on the matters he excludes from his statement of religion in *Ethical Studies.* Yet his object in all contexts is essentially the same: to define the religious consciousness and to distinguish it from the moral consciousness in both its social and cultural aspects.

In pursuing this end, he says things which to the unreflecting pious may appear hostile to religion, as when he differentiates religion from superstition and other savage attitudes which to his mind adulterate the modern religious consciousness, or when he distinguishes between the instrumentalities of religion and its end. But in all this his remarks are directed not against religion, but against its abuses and excesses. "Neither against the clergy, nor the sacraments, nor private devotion am I saying one word; and the reader who so understands me altogether misunderstands me."[181] So to those who insist on "sound sense and clear thinking" it may seem that to deny ultimate theoretic truth to religious ideas is in effect to abandon religion. Yet in Bradley's view religion is a necessity.

Religion is a specific discipline giving expression to one side of human nature. At the same time it is the nature of the religious consciousness to view its object as the complete reality. This, Bradley thinks, is a confused attempt to grasp the Absolute in religion; for, though "there is nothing more real than what comes in religion," religion "is not final and ultimate."[182]

It may be said, in general, that Bradley stops with philosophy. He writes as a philosopher; and when he treats of religion, he writes as a philosopher of religion, not as a religious philosopher. Philosophy does not create its subjects; it starts with what is given. The religious consciousness, with Bradley, is a fact, or, as he and Eliot might say, it exists. And the aim of philosophy is not to explain the fact away or to teach an old religion or to create a new one; the aim is to understand the given fact.[183]

According to Bradley, philosophy is a narrower discipline than religion. It is concerned with intellectual truth and satisfaction, whereas religion is the attempt to express the good in all its aspects, and as such it embraces every human excellence. In this respect, it is wider and higher than philosophy. But where it is a question of knowledge, philosophy stands higher than religion. But philosophy does not contradict religion— so long as religion does not offer its special truths as ultimate ones. Since there is a difference between the sense of a doctrine as a working idea and its theoretical sense, we have two different ways of understanding.[184]

From the point of view of philosophy, God is an object of the religious consciousness, and outside that consciousness God has no meaning. The object of the theoretic consciousness is truth, which is merely the ideal aspect of the Absolute. The Absolute is not God, nor is it a substitute for God; it is not an object of worship. If we bring the general idea of the Absolute before our minds, we are not having a religious experience, though we may be satisfying the mystical side of our nature.[185]

Philosophy and religion, then, are distinct disciplines; moreover, neither is the completion of the other.

> Philosophy . . . is itself but appearance. It is but one appearance among others, and, if it rises higher in one respect, in other ways it certainly stands lower. And its weakness lies, of course, in the fact that it is barely theoretical. Philosophy may be *made* more undoubtedly, and incidentally it *is* more; but its essence clearly must be confined to intellectual activity. It is therefore but a one-sided and inconsistent appearance of the Absolute. And, so far as philosophy is religious, to that extent we must allow that it has passed into religion, and has ceased, as such, any longer to be philosophy. I do not suggest to those who, dissatisfied with religious beliefs, may have turned seriously to metaphysics, that they will not find there what they seek. But they will not find it there, or anywhere else, unless they have brought it with them. Metaphysics has no special connexion with genuine religion, and neither of these two appearances can be regarded as the perfection of the other. The completion of each is not to be found except in the Absolute.[186]

If religion is not the Absolute, is not final and ultimate, what, "common sense" asks, is the result in practice?

> That, I reply at once, is not my business; and insistence on such a question would rest on a hurtful prejudice. The task of the metaphysician is to inquire into ultimate truth, and he cannot be called on to consider anything else, however important it may be. We have but little notion in England of freedom either in art or in science. Irrelevant appeals to practical results are allowed to make themselves heard. And in certain regions of art and science this sin brings its own punishment; for we fail through timidity and through a want of singleness and sincerity. That a man should treat of God and religion in order merely to understand them, and apart from the influence of some other consideration and inducement, is to many of us in part unintelligible, and in part also shocking. And hence English thought on these subjects, where it has not studied in a foreign school, is theoretically worthless.[187]

Bradley is aware that this position is likely to strike "common sense" as evasive if not dishonest. It does not answer to the demand of "common sense" for a universe of clear-cut divisions and fixed points of reference. Nor is "common sense" inclined to recognize the independence of philosophy and art or the limitations of morality and religion; it tends rather to extend the conclusions arrived at in these last disciplines to provinces outside their competence, indifferent to the conflicts thus engendered among human needs and to the violence done alike to philosophy and art and morality and religion.

Bradley sees no likelihood of reconciling the outlook of metaphysics with that of "common sense." The most that can be hoped for, he thinks, is rational discussion of an insoluble problem. The chief obstacle

to such discussion is the confusion which arises from
the failure to distinguish the essential from the incidental in religion. The clarification of such confusion is a philosophic task, involving both an understanding of the historical facts of religion and a
consistent view of the nature of reality, truth, and
goodness. Apart from such a view, we confuse the essential and the unessential, theory and practice, religion and science.[188]

Does Bradley's position satisfy Eliot? Let us hear
first from Bradley what the terms are. The chief obstacles, he says, to receiving his view of religion are
the demand for theoretical consistency in religion and
the doctrine of individualism. We will consider these
separately.

Of the first of these conditions, Bradley says:

> No one is likely to content himself with the doctrine
> which I advocate, if he believes that there is no truth
> except the truth which is self-consistent and ultimate, and
> that this absolute truth is required for religion. And the
> idea that Absolutism, as I understand it, can fully warrant
> relative and inconsistent truths, will to many seem even
> monstrous.[189]

Here, for example, is Bradley's reply to those who
are distressed by his notion that the object of religion,
the supreme good, is real and yet remains to be realized:

> Now nothing is easier than for a one-sided reflection
> to rush in with a cry for clearness and consistency, and

to apply its favourite "either-or". "*If* real, how realize? *If* realize, then not real.*" We, however, must not allow ourselves to give way to the desire for drawing conclusions, but have to observe the facts; and we see that the religious consciousness refuses the dilemma. It holds to both one and the other, and to one because of the other; and pronounces such reflections irreligious.[190]

Here, for comparison, is Eliot, in "Thoughts After Lambeth":

To put it frankly, . . . the Roman view in general seems to me to be that a principle must be affirmed without exception; and that thereafter exceptions can be dealt with, without modifying the principle. The view natural to the English mind, I believe, is rather that a principle must be framed in such a way as to include all allowable exceptions. It follows inevitably that the Roman Church must profess to be fixed, while the Anglican Church must profess to take account of changed conditions . . . . [The Roman way] is another conception of human nature and of the means by which, on the whole, the greatest number of souls can be saved; but the difference goes deep . . . . The admission of inconsistencies, sometimes ridiculed as indifference to logic and coherence, of which the English mind is often accused, may be largely the admission of inconsistencies inherent in life itself, and of the impossibility of overcoming them by the imposition of a uniformity greater than life will bear.[191]

Here is Eliot again, in *Notes towards the Definition of Culture:*

Hence, for the purposes of this essay, I am obliged to maintain two contradictory propositions: that religion and culture are aspects of one unity, and that they are two different and contrasted things.[192]

And in the Note to "Dante":

In short, both the view I have taken in this essay, and the view which contradicts it, are, if pushed to the end, what I call heresies (not, of course, in the theological, but in a more general sense). Each is true only within a limited field of discourse, but unless you limit fields of discourse, you can have no discourse at all. Orthodoxy can only be found in such contradictions, though it must be remembered that a pair of contradictions may *both* be false, and that not all pairs of contradictions make up a truth.[193]

Eliot, then, is not among those who find it monstrous that there should be relative and inconsistent truths. Indeed, orthodoxy presupposes the existence of such truths, and is relative to them. Orthodoxy takes the form of a unity of opposed and unreduced elements, and heresy that of extreme and exclusive positions.

This view of things is not, of course, peculiar to Bradley. It is, in the first place, Greek, then scholastic, and, in attenuated form, Hegelian. It is, it may be said, the view characteristic of metaphysics, understood not as a particular doctrine, but as a mode of thought, which, starting with what is given, seeks to do justice to all sides of life.

The typical Greek view of reality takes into account mind and matter. These are elements of both man and the universe. Nature, human and external, is universal as well as particular, comprising immaterial and sensible realities. Thus the very nature of things harbors oppositions and contradictions. The Greeks thought it was possible, by subordinating matter to mind, the animal to the rational, the transient to the permanent (the divine), to attain a harmony which, within limits, might satisfy the needs of the whole man.

The basis of Catholic orthodoxy is faith in the sacred character of biblical events, especially the redemption of the Son of Man, body as well as soul. Aristotle's doctrine of the individual as a composite of form and matter came virtually pat to the hands of theologians seeking philosophic articulation of this central point of faith. But even in the patristic age, when stoicism and neo-Platonism supplied Christian thinkers with their ideas, the church perforce regarded the extremes of spiritualism and materialism as heresies. Patristic and scholastic theology sought a resolution of the opposition of body and mind in a supernatural principle which is distinct from and yet informs both sense and intelligence.

In modern idealism, the ancient oppositions reappear as spirit and nature, now reconciled by the Absolute. With Bradley, relations are contradictions; and his totalities, in their various stages and degrees, are syntheses of contradictory elements—the thesis and antithesis, as it were, of Hegel's dialectic. The dualism with Bradley is that of existence and idea—and existence in effect means feeling. The root of disharmony is implicit in feeling, so that there is an inherent defect at the very source of life. The defect, moreover, is ineradicable. Our practical activity, our philosophy, our art—all are special developments with the object of making good the original instability; and all, by their self-contradictions, are doomed to failure. Life is thus radically imperfect, marked by unrest and discontent. "Everything in life," says Bradley, "is imperfect and seeks beyond itself an absolute fulfillment of itself." "On this point the verdict of those who know most of life has been passed long ago, and, later or sooner, this finding must at some time have come home to us as true."[194]

That, very likely, is part of what Eliot means when he speaks of Bradley as being in the Greek tradition. Bradley, like the Greeks, Eliot says, offers a balanced view of things, the result of "maturity and study and thought." He had a large store of wisdom. He saw life in its "complexity and connections." He looked at the world with "scepticism and uncynical disillusion." "And scepticism and disillusion are a useful equipment for religious understanding; and of that Bradley had a share too."[195]

Bradley, says Eliot, is "thoroughly empirical, much more empirical than the philosophies that he opposed." He is empirical, I take it, in the metaphysical sense: he starts with what is given, retains all the terms of experienced fact, pursues their implications to the end, and stops with skepticism—not a positive doctrine, but reservation of judgment. This, according to Eliot, is the "orthodox" mode of thought, the one-sided views Bradley opposed being "heresies." The one endeavors to hold on to all sides of experience, whatever its perplexities and contradictions, trusting reason while recognizing its limitations, and hence in matters human content with incompleteness. The other seeks naive resolutions in dogmatic oversimplifications. The one, Eliot thinks, is wise, supple, patient, civilized; the other immature, inflexible or fluid, cranky, crude.

The other condition Bradley lays down is the doctrine of individualism. He says:

We encounter here the main hindrance to the adoption of a view of religion such as that which I have accepted. On the assumption that individual men, yourself and myself, are real each in his own right, to speak of God as having reality in the religious consciousness, I agree, is nonsense. God must be another independent individual, and, if not that, is not real at all. On the other hand, unless this whole assumption is rejected or ignored, the essential content of the religious consciousness must, I submit, be lost or denied. And the independent reality of the individual, when we examine it, is in truth mere illusion. Apart from the community what are separate men? It is the common mind within him which gives reality to the human being, and taken by himself, whatever else he is, he is not human. When he opposes himself to the community it is still the whole which lives and moves in discord within him, for by himself he is an abstraction without life or force. If this is true of the social consciousness in its various forms, it is true certainly no less of that common mind which is more than social. In art, in science and in religion, the individual by himself remains still an abstraction. The finite minds that in and for religion form one spiritual whole, have indeed in the end no visible embodiment, and yet, except as members in an invisible community, they are nothing real. For religion in short, if the one indwelling Spirit is removed, there are no spirits left.[196]

In his essay on Bradley, Eliot quotes the following passage from *Ethical Studies:*

> How can the human-divine ideal ever be my will? The answer is, Your will it never can be as the will of your private self, so that your private self should become wholly good. To that self you must die, and by faith be made one with that ideal. You must resolve to give up your will, as the mere will of this or that man, and you must put your whole self, your entire will, into the will of the divine. That must be your one self, as it is your true self; that you must hold to both with thought and will, and all other you must renounce.[197]

In his gloss on this passage Eliot makes three points. The first is that Bradley's position is to be distinguished from that of Arnold and Irving Babbitt. "The distinction," Eliot says, "is not between a 'private self' and a 'public self' or a 'higher self,' it is between the individual as himself and no more, a mere numbered atom, and the individual in communion with God. The distinction is clearly drawn between man's 'mere will' and 'the will of the Divine.' " Secondly, he observes that "there is one direction in which these words—and, indeed, Bradley's philosophy as a whole— might be pushed, which would be dangerous; the direction of diminishing the value and dignity of the individual, of sacrificing him to a Church or a State." Thirdly, illustrating Arnold's inconsistency, he says: "But *if* there is a 'will of God,' as Arnold, in a hasty moment, admits, then some doctrine of Grace must be admitted too; or else the 'will of God' is just the same inoperative benevolence which we have all now and then received—and resented—from our fellow human beings. In the end it is a disappointment and a cheat."

Eliot locates Bradley's position between that of Arnold and, it may be said, that of Augustine and Aquinas. As to the danger in Bradley's position, it can hardly be said to lie on the surface. The general effect of his Absolutism is a system of checks and balances, of divided authority. We err, says Bradley, "when we attempt to set up any one aspect of our nature as supreme, and to regard the other aspects merely as conducive and as subject to its rule." Bradley indeed issues a warning similar to Eliot's, though with him the danger proceeds from another direction. The pursuit of consistency in religion, he says, leads to "fatal one-sidedness," "an over-emphasis on the universal aspect, and with this will come the belittling of what is individual and personal."[198]

The danger, so far as Eliot is concerned, lies in Bradley's denial of the independent reality of the self and God. This is the chief reservation in Eliot's adaptation of Bradley. He adjusts Bradley to a doctrine of the individual which is neither that of utilitarianism nor that of Absolutism.

Eliot's gloss on Bradley is typical of the sort of thing we find throughout his work. And it illustrates the difficulty of distinguishing the elements in his thought and his way of adjusting them. The point I wish to make here is that Eliot's rejection of Bradley's doctrine of the individual—which stands or falls with the Absolute—is not a belated reaction to his entrance into the English Church. It is earlier than that, as may be seen from his two articles in *The Monist* (1916), and from the quotation from Aristotle in "Tradition and the Individual Talent."

CHAPTER 7
SCHOLASTICISM

ELIOT'S ARTICLES IN *The Monist* are entitled "The Development of Leibniz's Monadism" and "Leibniz's Monads and Bradley's Finite Centers."[199] The articles show more than a knowledge of Leibniz and Bradley; they show a knowledge of Aristotle and scholasticism, and an admiration for scholastic thinkers. It is not pragmatists or idealists who speak, as Eliot does, of the scholasticism of the seventeenth century as "attenuated" and "degenerate" (for the "modern" mind it is all sterile) , or who would praise Leibniz for having a mind "clear and cold, the mind of a doctor of the church." Of course, being instructed in philosophy, Eliot can admire technical excellence whatever the content of the philosophy. But there is clearly more to it than that.

The two articles in *The Monist* are properly philosophic. The article on Leibniz deals mainly with the genesis of Leibniz's theory of the monad, but it also offers a criticism of the philosophic validity of the theory as distinguished from its theological and scientific aspects. Eliot's "motive" in this undertaking is clear. The point "of capital importance," he says, is that "one finds the acceptance of the problem of substance, transmitted from Aristotle through the form which the school had given it. In some ways diametrically in opposition with Aristotle, this scholastic view of substance which Leibniz held is yet an Aristotelian inheritance." Again, "the interest lies in Leibniz's saturation with the Aristotelian tradition." Leibniz, in the philosophic aspect of his theory, "is nearer to the Middle Ages, nearer to Greece, and yet nearer to us, than are men like Fichte and Hegel." Though Leibniz's metaphysical theory "falls apart," the significance of his work is that he "restored to life in a new form the doctrines of Plato and Aristotle." So the significance of Bradley is that "the tendency of his labours is to bring British philosophy closer to the Greek tradition." The difference, again, between Donne and Andrewes is that the latter is "the more mediaeval, because he is the more pure, and because his bond was with the Church, with tradition." And Marvell's best verse is "the product of European, that is to say Latin, culture." Eliot evinces the same fundamental interest in 1916, 1921, and 1926.[200]

Leibniz, according to Eliot, substitutes the concept of force for the Aristotelian form. A monad is an animated force which is contrasted with its states. But, Eliot thinks, there is no clear principle of distinction between force and its states. Its states are conceived both as material changes and as modes of expression in perception, feeling, and thought. Force and its states are simply the internal and external aspects of "an animated atom," a particular existence, exerting its activity at a point in time and space. Leibniz's monad, according to Eliot, is an explanation of the principle of matter based on the theory of dynamics and the feeling for activity. With his notion of this materialistic atom, Leibniz combines, unsuccessfully, a theory of the soul derived from theology and an idealistic metaphysics largely influenced by Descartes and based on self-consciousness. "Theology and physics," Eliot says, "join forces (so to speak) to rob metaphysics of its due."

In "Leibniz's Monads and Bradley's Finite Centers," Eliot takes Bradley's finite center and soul to be the counterpart of Leibniz's monad; and this is but one instance, according to him, of a general resemblance between these two philosophies. When treating of Leibniz, he singles out the materialistic aspect of the monad. When dealing with Bradley, he directs his criticism at the extreme idealistic aspects of Bradley's thought, and at similar aspects in Leibniz. "The Absolute," he says, "responds only to an imaginary demand of thought, and satisfies only an imaginary demand of feeling." It "dissolves at a touch into its constituents." The universe of Bradley, like that of Leibniz, is an ideal construction resting on faith. So, too, Bradley's self is "an ideal and largely a practical construction" in space and time. Further, the soul, with Bradley, differs from the finite center in not being identical with its states. But change, the activity of the soul, is not due to any agency outside the states of the soul themselves. Nor can one distinguish here between grades of soul according to faculty. Further, the same soul is from one point of view "a world in itself" and from another only "the function of a physical organism." Finally, with Bradley, as with Leibniz, internal and external—spirit and matter—are not adjectives qualifying different contents within the same world, but simply represent different points of view. Bradley's soul, like Leibniz's monad, reduces to points of view.

Eliot is concerned in these papers with the problem of substance and with its treatment in two notable philosophies in the European tradition. Leibniz, Eliot observes, stands between ancient and modern philosophy, pointing in both directions. He remains for Eliot "disquieting and dangerous," for he represents "no one tradition, no one civilization." Here is a philosophy with the most various possibilities of development, but what it opened the way to was not a re-creation of substantialism, but psychologism, idealism (in the modern sense), and logical positivism.

Aristotle, who inherited the problem of substance from Plato, did not, according to Eliot, succeed in resolving it, nor did he pretend to have done so. Aristotle's treatment of the problem, Eliot says, is incoherent, vague, and difficult. But there is this, among other things, to be said for him: though he fails to resolve his problem, he holds on to the terms involved in it. In this he is unlike modern philosophers who vacillate between idealism and materialism. He retains both particulars and universals, matter and form. He views the individual as a composite of form and matter, holding these two opposed principles to be relative and irreducible elements of a concrete reality.

The notion of substance is elusive. It is both difficult in itself and unfamiliar. Between us and it, so to speak, there is a large gap; for, as Eliot observes, the problem of matter and form turns up in modern thought as that of matter and spirit, and these are not corresponding sets of terms. We tend to think of matter and spirit as the external and internal aspects of a particular existence. There is the dichotomy of Descartes, with spirit as self-consciousness on one side and extended matter on the other. With others, all is spirit or all is matter. Lately we speak of a set of events which from one point of view is physical and from another mental; or we speak of the mind as a "fund" of organic experiences.

At any rate, the scholastics, like Aristotle, thought of substance and accidents as relative to each other, the two constituting a composite existence. Substance is to accidents as essence to existence or as soul to its states or activity. It is something of a relief to learn that, as Maurice De Wulf expresses it, the concept of substance is an idea "resulting from reasoning."[201] That is to say, the existence of the soul as a substance is based on an inference drawn from the activity of the soul. "It is only in fact by their operations," says Etienne Gilson, "that substances are known, and, conversely, operations are not to be explained except by substances." And with this supposition—that "every distinct operation supposes a distinct substance"[202] —we arrive at the notion of causality and sufficient reason. For where there is activity, there must be something that is active; and since activity *is* reality, the substance which is active is real. The inference, however, establishes only the existence of the soul; it does not testify to its nature. It tells us that the soul is and must be, not what it is.[203]

The respect of the schoolmen for Aristotle, as everyone knows, was very great. Scholastics employed his terms and principles, and they sought, whenever possible, to find a basis for their conclusions in his text. On the other hand, the religious spirit influenced their philosophy as it influenced every other aspect of medieval life—art, for example. As De Wulf and Gilson explain it, the scholastics often go beyond, modify, and improve on Aristotle.

For Aristotle, Eliot observes, substance is, in the main, "the form by which the matter is some definite thing." With organic beings, form is the soul of the body, the source and principle of its activity—form and matter constituting a substantial individual. Further, there is a form or soul common to the members of each species. Aristotle, according to Eliot, sometimes speaks as though the form of the species, a universal, became in each person a particular form, which constitutes the individuality of the person. This would appear to be a contradiction. But, in general, Aristotle does not hold that there is a particular form for each individual. What, then, distinguishes the individual members of a species from one another? Aristotle's answer is that the matter which combines with the form to constitute the individual is the principle of individuation.[204]

According to De Wulf and Gilson, this answer to

the problem did not satisfy the scholastics. To assign
the principle of individuation to matter (even formed
matter) is to make what is unique to each individual
extrinsic, accidental, and perishable. It suggests that
the form, the universal, is the important thing; this,
being a substance, is perdurable. But the individual,
as a substantial being, does not endure. Individuals
are of less importance than the species. Aquinas accepted, with a slight modification, Aristotle's principle
of individuation; but he made a distinction between
the principle of individuation and the principle of
individuality. The individuality of a being com-
pounded of matter and form is due to the form or
soul. The body, though it differentiates one individual
from another, is, apart from the soul, mere potenti-
ality. It is the soul that gives the composite being
activity and hence reality; the soul is the unifying
principle of the whole man.

Matter, then, is the principle of individuation, but
the soul is the principle of individuality—that is, a
being undivided in himself and divided from all
else, in virtue of being a concrete substance taken as
a whole.[205] Moreover, every human being is not only
an individual; he is also a personality. The accepted
medieval definition of a human person is that of
Boethius: "an individual substance of a rational
nature."[206] This means that the essence of the human
soul is intellect. The intellect is the root of personality
—the life of the spirit in its practical and theoretical
activity. The intellect is not man, for men have other
operations. Yet it is the intellect which informs and
unifies all the operations of man. It is the whole man
who thinks. The intellect itself, as substance, is dis-

tinguished from its activity. It acts not directly, but through the medium of its powers and faculties. Thus it remains one and the same throughout all its diverse activity. It is a self-identical, impenetrable, and immaterial substance or essence.

This, in some of its points, is the scholastic doctrine of the nature and reality of the individual. It is a philosophic doctrine, and, more particularly, a metaphysics of substance. It makes the substantiality of intellect the basis of human individuality and personality. The intellect, too, is the basis of liberty and immortality.[207] If it were not for the intellect, men would be things subject to natural forces. As it is, intellect puts men in possession of a principle of free determination, a principle of learning and discrimination, and thereby makes it possible for them to choose their own destiny. And since the intellect is, by definition, immaterial, it is the reason of immortality. Finally, the individual only is real. The State is not real in the sense that the individual is, for the unity of the State is not physical and internal, but ideal and external. The individual only is something in and for himself. States perish, but individuals are eternal.[208]

Scholastic philosophy is completed by scholastic natural theology, which is but the final extension of its principles of philosophic reasoning. The chief principles here are those of efficient causality and contradiction. If activity and substance are mutually explanatory, there must be a cause of the activity in the universe, and this cause must be a substance. Further, substance, though the cause of activity, is independent of it. De Wulf says:

It all comes then to this: if any fact is real, the totality of things, without which the reality of that fact would be compromised, is no less real. It follows, therefore, that scholastic philosophy demonstrates God's existence by making His existence a necessary condition of the explanation of reality. Accordingly, from the standpoint of metaphysics, He exists only for the world. Hence God is not, as one might suppose, a further mystery requiring explanation, in addition to the general mystery of the world.[209]

There can be little doubt that the point of view implicit in Eliot's criticism of Leibniz and Bradley is that of scholasticism. We must suppose that Eliot at one time was engaged in what Bradley calls "a sincere metaphysical endeavour," and that the endeavor ended in theoretical skepticism, which Bradley defines as "the mere denial of any known satisfactory doctrine, together with the personal despair of any future attainment."[210] Wisdom, Eliot says, consists largely of "scepticism and uncynical disillusion," and "scepticism and disillusion are a useful equipment for religious understanding."

In a talk on "Christianity and Communism," Eliot says:

> Towards any profound conviction one is borne gradually, perhaps insensibly over a long period of time, by what Newman called "powerful and concurrent reasons". . . . At some moment or other, a kind of crystallisation occurs, in which appears an element of *faith* not strictly definable from any reason or combination of reasons. I am not speaking, mind you, of conversion to Christian faith only, but of conversion in general; . . . . In my

own case, I believe that one of the reasons was that the Christian scheme seemed to me the only one which would work. I hasten to add that this is not a reason for be-lieving; it is a tenable hypothesis to maintain that there is *no* scheme which will work. That was simply the re-moval of any reason for believing in anything else, the erasure of a prejudice, the arrival at the scepticism which is the preface to conversion. . . . Among other things, the Christian scheme seemed the only possible scheme which found a place for values which I must maintain or perish (and belief comes first and practice second), . . .[211]

Theoretical skepticism, according to Bradley, serves at least "as a deliverance from spiritual oppression." But, he says:

Such a result, where there is nothing better, may be welcome, and yet such a result is not in general enough . . . . There is a desire deep-seated in our nature for what we call truth, and for the intelligent and rational justifi-cation of our best instincts. We want and we require in short some kind of working creed, and this requirement is hardly met by any mere collection of working ideas. And where there are no metaphysics, or where meta-physics have led to no positive result, such a doctrine apparently would have to rest on what we call religion, individual or general.

There is, I should say, a need, and there is even a certain demand, for a new religion. We want a creed to recognize and justify in due proportion all human interests, and at the same time to supply the intellect with that to which it can hold with confidence. Whether we shall get this new religion, and, if so, how, whether by modification of what exists or in some other way, I am unable to surmise. But it is not, so far as I can see, in the power of philosophy to supply this general demand. And I must doubt the possibility of a religious doctrine able in the end to meet our metaphysical requirement of ultimate consistency. All that, in my opinion, we can reasonably desire, is on one side a general faith, and on the other side such a critical philosophy as would be able in some sense to justify and to support this faith. I think, that is (to use a word perhaps anticipated by the reader), that any positive metaphysical doctrine must remain "esoteric", while a religion condemned to be esoteric is but a refuge amid general destitution. Therefore a religious belief founded otherwise than on metaphysics, and a metaphysics able in some sense to justify that creed, seems to me what is required to fulfil our wishes. And though this fulfilment is a thing which I cannot myself expect to see, and though the obstacles in its way are certainly great, on the other hand I cannot regard it as impossible.[212]

Eliot's philosophic quest appears to be gradually superseded by a position based on religious dogma and an ethics determined by dogma. Philosophically, he holds to the scholastic version of the soul. For the rest, his working ideas and attitudes are in the main derived from Bradley. That is the general form and composition of his thought.

Eliot tends to explain things to himself in terms of Bradley's thought and frequently in his very language or some adaptation of it. For instance, what Eliot tells us of his inner history is virtually given in terms of Bradley. According to Bradley, "faith in general" goes beyond mere feeling or sensible perception. It excludes knowledge grounded in ideas or verified in facts. Though not "knowledge proper," it "implies some kind of believing and knowing"; "the non-logical overcoming from within of doubt as to an idea, or the similar prevention of such doubt, appears, so far, to be the general essence of faith."[213] "Doubt and uncertainty," says Eliot, "are merely a variety of belief."[214]

Here, for good measure, are some instances of Eliot's use of Bradley.

Eliot:

The majority of people live below the level of belief or doubt.[215]

elitism ugh!

Bradley:

If you descend . . . below a certain intellectual level, the word "faith" becomes inapplicable.[216]

In his article on Leibniz, Eliot says:

But his transmigration of human souls is muddled by the identification of soul, in the sense of personality, with the animated point; of the core of feeling of the self with the force of which it is predicated.[217]

The "soul, in the sense of personality," I take for scholasticism; but "the core of feeling of the self" is surely Bradley:

The inner core of feeling . . . is the foundation of the self.[218]

In "John Bramhall," Eliot says:

> I have asserted that Hobbes's psychological analysis of
> the human mind has no rational connection with his
> theory of the State. But it has, of course, an emotional
> connection; one can say that both doctrines belong nat-
> urally to the same temperament.[219]

This is plainly a draft on Bradley, who writes:

> Or he [the individual] may rather have several worlds
> without rational unity, conjoined merely by co-existence
> in his own personality. And this separation and discon-
> nectedness (we may fail to observe) is, in some degree,
> normal.[220]

Here, with the order reversed, is another draft.
Bradley:

> If, in the second place again, we are not clear about the
> nature of scientific truth, can we rationally deal with any
> alleged collision between religion and science? We shall,
> in fact, be unable to say whether there is any collision or
> none; or again, supposing a conflict to exist, we shall be
> entirely at a loss how to estimate its importance. And
> our result so far is this. If English theologians decline
> to be in earnest with metaphysics, they must obviously
> speak on some topics, I will not say ignorantly, but at
> least without having made a serious attempt to gain
> knowledge.[221]

Eliot, in "Thoughts After Lambeth," quotes the following passage from the Report:

> Perhaps most noteworthy of all, there is much in the
> scientific and philosophic thinking of our time which

provides a climate more favorable to faith in God than has existed for generations.

He then offers this comment:

> I cannot help wishing that the bishops had consulted some of the able theologians and philosophers within the Church (such as Professor A. E. Taylor, who published an excellent article on the God of Whitehead, in *Theology*) before they had bestowed this benediction on our latest popular ramp of best sellers.

Eliot, in the same essay:

> My objection therefore is not to the admission of dissenters to the Altar . . . but to the propagation of this practice before theological justification has been expounded. Possibly theology is what Bradley said philosophy was: "the finding of bad reasons for what we believe upon instinct"; I think it may be the finding of good reasons for what we believe upon instinct; but if the Church of England cannot find these reasons, and make them intelligible to the more philosophically trained among the faithful, what can it do?[222]

To make an end, here is Bradley:

> Where you have a felt whole, as felt, or where you have a non-relational unity, as in a work of art, there, so far, you need not ask 'why'. . . . The case is different where, by analysis or otherwise, the self-contained unity has been lost. Wherever the oneness of 'what' and 'that' has perished before us, or has been destroyed by reflection and analysis, and wherever we seek to reunite these aspects not really but ideally, we have a demand for a 'reason'.[223]

And Eliot:

> One of the surest of tests is the way in which a poet borrows. Immature poets imitate; mature poets steal; bad poets deface what they take, and good poets make it into something better, or at least something different. The good poet welds his theft into a whole of feeling which is unique, utterly different from that from which it was torn; the bad poet throws it into something which has no cohesion. A good poet will usually borrow from authors remote in time, or alien in language, or diverse in interest.[224]

Eliot is steeped in Bradley. But there is another aspect of his relation to Bradley, the explanation of which is again supplied by Bradley:

> For whether there is progress or not, at all events there is change; and the changed minds of each generation will require a difference in what has to satisfy their intellect. Hence there seems as much reason for new philosophy as there is for new poetry. In each case the fresh production is usually much inferior to something already in existence; and yet it answers a purpose if it appeals more personally to the reader. What is really worse may serve better to promote, in certain respects and in a certain generation, the exercise of our best functions. And that is why, so long as we alter, we shall always want, and shall always have, new metaphysics.[225]

Bradley offers more modern weapons than scholasticism, and more penetrating ones than Arnold, for controverting the "Utilitarian mind." Finally, there is Eliot's assertion that we can distinguish the beliefs of the poet from those of the man. How this is to be done with Dante, for instance, Eliot neither explains nor demonstrates. Yet we have gained some notion how it is to be done with Eliot.

CHAPTER 8

AN IMPERSONAL
THEORY OF POETRY

IN "TRADITION AND THE Individual Talent" Eliot offers
an "impersonal theory of poetry." Its practical object
is to direct attention upon the poetry rather than the
poet. The theory has two parts: the poet's relation to
the past, and his relation to his poetry.

The poet, he says, in virtue of having acquired the
"historical sense," stands in a subtle relation to the
entire body of poetry which precedes him. Further,
he can be fully understood and appreciated only when
he is set within this body of poetry, which is conceived
as an ideal order. And this is meant as "a principle of
aesthetic, not merely historical criticism."

Again, poetry, Eliot says, is not properly to be
understood as the expression of personal emotion; it

is a working up or concentration of impressions and experiences in ways which are peculiar and diverse and which do not happen consciously or with deliberation. What the poet has to express is not a "personality," but "a particular medium."

It is the practice, Eliot observes, to value in a poet's work the part which is individual. But, he says, if we approach a poet without "this prejudice," we shall find that the most individual parts of his work may be those which he owes to the poets of the past, and this so far as he has acquired the "historical sense," which is a sense of "the timeless and of the temporal together."

He says:

> The point of view which I am struggling to attack is perhaps related to the metaphysical theory of the substantial unity of the soul: for my meaning is, that the poet has, not a "personality" to express, but a particular medium, which is only a medium and not a personality, in which impressions and experiences combine in peculiar and unexpected ways.

A few paragraphs later he employs a quotation from Aristotle as an epigraph:

> Mind is, no doubt, something more divine and impassable.

And he declares that he proposes to halt "at the frontier of metaphysics or mysticism."

The near presence of the two passages in the same essay has led commentators to assume that Eliot is repudiating a metaphysical theory of the substantial unity of the soul. And indeed he is. But it is not the Aristotelian-scholastic theory he is repudiating; it is the theory of Leibniz.

Leibniz's theory of substance, Eliot says, though indirectly derived from Aristotle's, is quite different from it. "If the form or principle of Aristotle were different in each man, this form would be Leibniz's soul." With Leibniz, not Aristotle, the soul is a monad, a simple, particular atom or unit, self-sufficient and impervious to change. This is the individual, the essence of the self, which is expressed in its states, the monad and its states being one and the same. And this has suggested, Eliot is saying, that personality is something simple and fixed, and that this is what is expressed in poetry.

"The view of Leibniz," Eliot says, "comes, *via* nominalism, out of Aristotle himself." But, according to Eliot, the mind with Aristotle is not a material atom conceived as a center of force. It is not a thing at all, Eliot says, but an operation—that is to say, a medium. Like a piece of platinum, it is impassable, but it is also, in one respect, divine, coming from without. Nor is Aristotle a nominalist; with him the particular apart from the universal is unintelligible. Again, neither Plato nor Aristotle, Eliot says, found reality "in each individual as a world apart. This is an instance of the differences between Leibniz and the Greeks." For the Greeks, "the human was the typically human, individual differences were not of scientific interest; for the modern philosopher individual differences were of absorbing importance."[226]

The poetic theory Eliot is attacking is commonly associated with Romanticism, literary and philosophic. The importance attached to personality is, in general, the consequence of the shift from the objective outlook of the classical world to the subjective outlook of the modern—a shift mediated by the Middle Ages. The change is reflected, in philosophy, by Descartes, who takes the thinking subject as the point of departure for his meditations; by Rousseau, who takes the feeling subject for the starting point of his; and by the German thinkers, starting with Kant, who make a self-conscious distinction between the subjective and the objective sides of life.

With this change, the self takes the center of the stage, and poetry comes to be regarded as the expression of the self—that is, in terms of imagination. The empiricists, who reject the concept of substance, think of the self as a complex of impressions held together by the principles of association. Though Kant also thinks the concept of substance inscrutable, he believes that the reduction of the self to a series of impressions distorts the character of conscious life. For him, the basic form of mental life is an activity of synthesis— ordering, combining, unifying; and this activity presupposes a unified consciousness. After Kant, the self is, in general, regarded as a unity which finds expression in its diverse activities, the individuality of the self being defined by its peculiar manner of ordering and unifying. Individuality comes to be viewed as interesting for its own sake; and the expression of individuality is thought to endow a work of art with its special value. As Pater, a late Romantic, states it, "the seal on a man's work of what is most inward and peculiar in his moods and manner of apprehension."[227]

In "The Function of Criticism" Eliot relates this shift in outlook to questions of poetry and criticism. The shift there appears as the issue of individualism and authority, the first represented by Romanticism and the second by Classicism and Catholicism. Eliot holds that these outlooks are incompatible and that the incompatibility extends to their respective attitudes towards art and criticism. He takes notice here of the transcendental element of Romantic philosophy, according to which the immanence of the Absolute in finite experience endows such experience with a universal value. But he does so only to dismiss it as a "form of pantheism," which, he says, is not European.[228] Hence it does not figure in his contrast of the Romantic and Classical-Catholic outlooks. As he represents these, the one is personal and subjective, and the other impersonal and objective. One regards literature as an aggregate of individual works, and finds the significance of such works in the personalities they reflect. The other views literature in terms of organic wholes, and finds the significance of individual works and authors in their relation to the system of which they are parts. In this last view, the poet and the critic give allegiance to something outside themselves: to the art of poetry and to the tradition of their country and Europe as a whole. What constitutes Europe as a distinct civilization is, first, its common ancestry in Greece, Rome, and Israel, and, in the more modern sense, the Christianity of the Middle

Ages.[229] It is this concept that Eliot refers to when he speaks of "the mind of Europe" and, in the narrower sense, of "tradition."

The idea of order in literature is an essential postulate of Eliot's poetics. In his view, it is the idea of literature as an ideal order that gives significance to the work of poet and critic. The alternative view is the idea of literature as an aggregate of works considered as expressing the individual differences of their authors. The order of literature, as Eliot conceives it, is that of an organic whole. The principle of the whole is the concept of poetry as a universal activity. Though the material of poetry is ever changing, the activity itself remains the same—a distinct function of human nature having as its object the evocation of a reality which does not change. Poetry exists in its particular embodiments, which, as conditioned by time and place, form a history of poetry. At the same time, its embodiments constitute an ideal order in virtue of their character as poetry. The order is exhibited, more or less, in its particular embodiments, and its particular embodiments find their significance in the measure in which they give expression to the order.

If a poet writes a really new poem, his work will cause a change, however slight, in the system of existing poems. If order is to persist, there must be a readjustment of the relations and values in respect to the principle of the whole. If a poem is really new, there is growth and adjustment. That follows from the idea of an organic whole. The principle of such a whole is the reciprocal relation of the parts: every part is both cause and effect—the leaves are the product of the rest of the tree, but they also support the rest of the tree.

⟨A new work leads to a revaluation of the past. In this respect, art is like any other formal discipline. Natural science, for example, is a readjusting system defined by a distinctive activity. A new work in physics, say, alters the relations and values of work done in the past. What would be the significance of Newton's work considered in abstraction from the activity of physics? Though Newton is an embodiment of that activity, the activity is something other than Newton; it has other embodiments, and all these find their significance in the activity. It is not, then, preposterous, Eliot says, "that the past should be altered by the present as much as the present is directed by the past."[230]

The order is the order of poetry. The poetry in a poem is what is contained in the synthesis of its parts; and that something is related to the poem as a universal to a particular. It is something which issues from the poetic process and is independent of the poet (as the work of scientists is independent of individual scientists). It is objective; it exists. If it did not exist, we could have no criticism. In aesthetic judgment, according to Eliot, we are concerned with emotion and its expression. This is something we directly perceive. But the ideal order of poetry is the implicit basis of judgment. Judgment involves a relation, a comparison, and hence we can compare two poems only by reference, implicit or explicit, to something common to both. To say of two poems that they are different, in quality, is to say that they are both poetry. If they were not both poetry, they could not be compared. That, I take it, is what Eliot means when he says: "It is a judgment, a comparison, in which two things are measured by each other."[231] That is also why comparison and analysis, the chief tools of the critic, "need only the cadavers on the table." But the critic must know what to compare. Further, no poet has his full significance by himself. He must be judged in relation to a historical order of poetry, national or European. Eliot illustrates the procedure in his practical criticism.

Eliot's notion of "the sense of tradition," of "the historical sense," is further complicated by the way in which he conceives the relation of past and present. The poet who acquires "the historical sense" is "conscious of his place in time" and of his time as "but the present moment of the past." In this view, the past is not external to the present. It is not the past of archaeology or of philology—a record of objects, events, ideas, institutions, or literary monuments classified according to types and periods and representing factual knowledge of bygone times. Nor is it the past which we reconstruct with the help of such knowledge and by an exercise of the historical imagination, projecting ourselves into other periods and re-enacting modes of thought and feeling other than our own. Eliot, of course, recognizes the value of such studies and exercises; they are part of his "programme for the *métier* of poetry." But it is not learning, however imaginative, that he has in mind when he speaks of "the historical sense." Indeed, what he means is the negation of what is commonly understood by history and scholarship, or, what is perhaps the same thing, the transcendence of these.

In his view, there is but one time, which is ever present; for there is no time apart from consciousness, and consciousness is always a present fact. Past and present are distinctions within time; they are not external to each other, as are the events by reference to which we date things. The poet lives in the present, and his awareness of the past is part of his present experience, so that past and present are together in a present moment of consciousness. Thus the past which lives in the present is the present moment of the past. The poet who acquires "the historical sense" is conscious "not of what is dead, but of what is already living."

This view of the relation of past and present, of time, very likely owes something to Bergson as well as to Bradley. But where there is no evidence to the contrary, the supposition of influence, I think, must be in favor of Bradley. For when Eliot takes things from others, his general practice is to interpret them in terms of Bradley. What is common to Bergson and Bradley is the notion of reality as immediate experience; and it is this common notion that gives rise to the general similarity in their views.

If reality is, in some sense, immediate experience, the past can be said to exist only if it is present. The present, with Bradley, is not time opposed to past and future. It is the negation of time. The present is a duration in which reality is directly apprehended. What is present is not *time*, but the content of consciousness, which is out of time. Consciousness as an event is in time, but its content is universal.

The present is an ideal construction based on feeling and perception; and this is also the character of the past: the past is an ideal construction based on present feeling and perception. Accordingly, as these change, the past, or our view of the past, changes. The past is relative to the changing present. If present feeling and perception do not support and enter into the extension of themselves which is the past, that past, says Bradley, has disappeared. Thus mere knowledge about the past is not apprehension of the past. Though ideas enter into it, the past as reality is apprehended in direct awareness.

Since time involves a relation of before and after, it is self-contradictory, and hence a mere appearance, which, apart from the Absolute, or a permanent reality otherwise conceived, is a meaningless abstraction. Like all appearances, says Bradley, it "directs us beyond itself" to "something higher in which it is included and transcended."[232]

These notions, as every reader of Eliot knows, have supplied him with a good deal of poetic substance.

So much, in this place, for the poet's relation to the past. The other part of the theory concerns the poet's relation to his poetry. To illustrate this relation, Eliot uses the analogy of a catalyst, likening the mind of the poet to a shred of platinum in the presence of two gases. The mind of the poet is represented as an agent for transmitting experiences, the elements of which are of two kinds, feelings and emotions. These are the material of poetry, and their fusion or combination is the poetic process. The material out of which the poetry is made may be drawn from the actual experience of the poet as man or it may have little to do with his practical experience. In either case the content of the poetry is a composition which is incommensurate with the historical experience of the poet. The result of the poetic process is a work of art, which is a new thing; and the difference between art and history is "always absolute." A poem is an "expression of *significant* emotion."

Eliot has a sense of his own time as well as of the past.[233] The elements of his aesthetics show the imprint of his period, though their form is of his own making.

His description of the poetic process might suggest a reliance on the empirical psychology of his time, which had taken up the notion of chemical combination. It certainly suggests, and his writings confirm, a knowledge of psychological theories. But with Eliot psychology is subject to correction and completion by philosophic analysis of the facts common to both disciplines. It is clear, I think, that he accepted Bradley's criticism of utilitarian psychology, and of the ethics based on that psychology. For instance, in *The Use of Poetry* his preference for Dryden's account of the imagination to the accounts of Addison, Wordsworth, and Coleridge is owing partly to the fact that these last incorporate Locke's notion of mind and Hartley's version of associationism. His strictures, to be sure, can be justified purely from the point of view of psychology; for psychology had become experimental, and empiricism had modified its earlier views. But it is not the empirical view of the self and of imagination as the expression of the self, old or new, that underlies Eliot's account of the poetic process.

In modern times, aesthetics has been treated as a philosophy of art and also as a science, a branch of psychology. German aesthetics from Kant to Hegel is philosophic: it treats of art in relation to the economy of life as a whole. English aesthetics offers, in the main, a description of imagination in terms of associationist psychology. Post-Hegelian theories of aesthetics, with exceptions like that of Croce, have been largely psychological. And after Darwin psychology is based on biology and physiology. The self and the imagination as the expression of the self come to be viewed in a new light, neither Lockian nor Kantian. In the new psychology of the late nineteenth and early twentieth centuries, these questions turn on the nature of complex states of mind. William James, in *Principles of Psychology* and *A Pluralistic Universe,* offers a convenient account of the issues dividing psychologists and of the philosophic implications of these issues.

One view, the "mind-dust" or "mind-stuff" theory —held by Spencer, Taine, and others—was suggested, says James, partly by the association of ideas and partly by the analogy of chemical compounds. This theory holds that "complex mental states are resultants of the self-compounding of simpler ones."[234] The chemical analogy, James argues, is misleading. *"All the 'combinations' which we actually know are EFFECTS, wrought by the units said to be 'combined' UPON SOME ENTITY OTHER THAN THEMSELVES.* Without this feature of a medium or vehicle, the notion of combination has no sense."[235] The scholastic view, James says, holds against all talk of "self-compounding" or "mental chemistry" or "psychic synthesis" which takes no account of a medium or vehicle other than and in addition to the units entering into combination.[236] In scholastic psychology, the soul or self or mind provides such a medium. The elements of experience produce effects on it, and the result is "a new and unique psychic creation."[237] As between these two theories, the evolutionary and the scholastic, the latter, says James, is logically the more intelligible. His own position, as psychologist rather than philosopher, though closer to the scholastic than the evolutionary, represents a *tertium quid*. Complex states of mind, he holds, are not compounds, but unitary forms of consciousness which are new facts. The units which are said to be 'combined,' when they come together, may be signals for the new "creation"; but the two are distinct, nor could one be deduced from the other. As a psychologist, he sees no need to invoke a soul or substantial mind to account for such creations. For one thing, a soul, assuming its existence, is not accessible to observation, but is something we infer from experiencing its states. It is only states of mind, phenomena, which are immediately known. And for empirical purposes, complex mental facts are adequately described as "pulses" of integral thought in the stream of consciousness.[238]

When James examined the philosophic implications of his psychology, he found that, if he held to the logic of identity, he had either to give up his psychology without a soul or revert to the spiritual agents of scholasticism—the idealist position he found the least intelligible of the three. Bergson, he says, showed him the way out of his dilemma, the solution being to forswear logic as a key to reality and to go over to the anti-intellectual position, empirical version.[239]

One general effect of Darwin's biological theory has been to invert the traditional relation between reason and emotion. Of course, something of such an inversion may be found before Darwin, though after Darwin it results in what is called anti-intellectualism. It marks a second stage in the critique of reason initiated by Kant; and it evokes, too, a second stage of reaction, which, like post-Kantian idealism, takes its direction from the new state of affairs.

The post-Darwinian assumption is a dualism of direct experience and thought. This assumption is accepted alike by positivists and anti-positivists, who draw opposite conclusions from it. Among anti-positivists—Nietzsche, in Germany; Croce, in Italy; Bergson, in France; Bradley, in England—reality is found in direct experience, not in the knowledge of external events as conceived by natural science. And reality is inexpressible in rational terms—though with Croce and Bradley reason enters into our judgments of reality, and with Bradley ideas represent the ideal aspect of reality.

According to Bergson, for example, to think as natural science thinks is to transform direct experience into an arbitrary set of concepts and relations; and these, though they enable us to manipulate the external world, tell us nothing of the inner reality of life, past or present. With Bergson, our direct experience is a fusion in time of states of mind; our past states are fused with our present ones in such a way as to constitute a unique creation. The emergent state of mind is an interpenetration of parts; the present includes the past, and both are present to intuition, not to reflection, and present only so long as intuition is active. Such a fusion of past and present in time distinguishes our inner life from the spatial organization of objects and events, of which, as biological creatures, we are a part. Here things are not fused, but external to one another, linked by a chain of cause and effect. This is the order of things symbolized by the conceptual knowledge of natural science, the entire value of which is pragmatic. According to Bergson, intuition[240] is not opposed to discursive thought, but completes it. It is the way in which we live our ideas rather than arrange them in abstract schemes serving the ends of action. Intuition is the organ of an empirical metaphysics which is ever incomplete; it is the apprehension of the reality—the thing-in-itself—which Kant declared to be inscrutable. And that reality is the insight into our existence as individuals enjoying and suffering time, change, and liberty.

In the aesthetics of this period, emotion is substituted for thought—moral ideas. This is in contrast to German aesthetics from Kant to Hegel, which, as Croce observes, remained at bottom rationalistic. Ribot,[241] for one, offers a psychological account of the new aesthetics, and Croce a philosophic one. Thus, for instance, Croce's object is to establish art as an autonomous activity, independent of morality, philosophy, and action. Art for him is an activity which is prior to thought and action, and as the most primitive form of consciousness, the basis of these, though not replaceable by them. Art is intuition, the perception of an image, a perception uncomplicated by concept or relation. The image produced by intuition issues from and is the expression of feeling, and that is what the reader apprehends. Poetry is thus an indivisible activity of the spirit, and of a given work we can only say that it is poetry or not poetry.

This is the milieu of Eliot's aesthetics. And it is impossible to read Eliot without thinking of any number of writers, of all kinds, who belong to this period. Yet I think his account of the poetic process is guided mainly by Bradley's analysis of experience. Bradley does not deny the fact of association; what he objects to is the empirical explanation of the fact, which is based on psychological atomism and on nominalism. With Bradley, association is a *mental* process. The connections between elements of whatever kind—perceptions, images, feelings—are mental: they are internal, not external; and the elements related are universals: they are elements which are identical in different contexts. Psychic elements as particular existences occur and perish, but their ideal aspect, their content, is reproduced in different contexts. It is the identity persisting through change and difference that constitutes the unity of the soul; such identity is also the basis of reasoning, and the basis of the extension of experience.[242]

Further, mental operations are present from the

start. Felt experience below explicit reasoning has the character of an ideal synthesis of differences. It brings together diverse elements in changing contexts, and hence involves selection and conjunction—in a word, abstraction. Thus the operations involved in the life of sensation, feeling, and perception are implicit modes of reasoning. Though not logical, they are intellectual. We judge, as Bradley has it, before we reason. We turn our sensations and feelings into objects of thought, and we manipulate these last, effecting comparisons, relations, and conjunctions. And all this is judgment. Inference—reasoning in the logical sense—does not begin with sense; it begins with an ideal object. Its basis is not sensuous, but intellectual, though ultimately, like judgment, it originates in feeling. It is difficult at certain stages of development to draw the line between these two types of intellectual activity—between sensation and thought. We must assume, Bradley holds, that the two types are coexistent, different aspects of one process.[243]

All this enters into the substance of Eliot's criticism, and provides the basis of his characteristic distinctions. For example, there is his notion of enjoying poetry—even in a language unknown to us—before understanding it. Enjoyment here would involve a judgment of perception, a perception of a sensuous whole as felt. Critical commentary would take the form of analysis and synthesis, two sides of one process. The critic would translate his feelings and perceptions into explicit thought, which, since its basis is sensuous, would be something less than reasoning. His object would be to make explicit the qualities and relations implicit in his enjoyment of the poetry. The result would be an ideal synthesis of his experience of the poem.

Again, take the phrase "objective correlative." According to Bradley, all experience is an objectification of feeling. A poem thus would represent one form of objectification—a form below that of explicit reasoning.

Take, further, the distinction between personal and impersonal. According to Bradley, everything which is given in experience, which is felt, is subjective and personal. At the same time, feeling is transmuted into objects of thought, and, on this side, as self-transcendent, is objective and impersonal. In general, any particular fact, any bit of personal experience, has a character of a certain kind (a "what" in addition to a "this") : it has, that is to say, a content (qualities and relations) , which, as ideal, points beyond the particular fact. Its specific meaning depends on the context to which it refers—aesthetic, moral, religious; and these spheres of reality are not subjective, but objective. In art as in science there is necessarily much that is not essential to the specific ends of these activities; and the irrelevant is, in the particular context, subjective and personal. Furthermore, what is irrelevant or personal in one context may not be so in another.[244] Thus Eliot:

> It would appear that 'literary appreciation' is an abstraction, and pure poetry a phantom; and that both in creation and enjoyment much always enters which is, from the point of view of 'Art,' irrelevant.[245]

The chief peculiarity of Eliot's description of the poetic process is the relation of "feelings" to "emotions." He says:

> It [a poem] may be formed out of one emotion, or may
> be a combination of several; and various feelings, inhering
> for the writer in particular words or phrases or images,
> may be added to compose the final result. Or great
> poetry may be made without the direct use of any emo-
> tion whatever: composed out of feelings solely.[246]

He offers examples and observations. We learn that
the murder of Agamemnon or the agony of Othello
gives an artistic effect closer to the actual experience
of murder and agony than does the episode of Paola
and Francesca to the actual experience of illicit love.
"In the *Agamemnon,* the artistic emotion approximates to the emotion of an actual spectator; in *Othello*
to the emotion of the protagonist himself."

The distinction between "feelings" and "emotions"
derives, I think, from Bradley, though the use Eliot
makes of it is original with him. An emotion, says
Bradley, such as anger or despondency, has two sides:
a felt side and an object-side, this last consisting of
cognitive elements, perceptions and ideas. The two
sides constitute "an emotional whole." Let us say that
this is the definite emotion the poet starts with. In
this whole, there are feelings lying in the background,
indefinite, unfocused, below or on the verge of consciousness. These latent feelings—the poet hardly
knows how or why—are translated, brought before his
mind, as perceptions and ideas (in words, phrases,
images). These, says Bradley, are special feelings
which, as translated, are united integrally though indirectly with the cognitive elements present from the

start, the whole emotion being one. And this synthesis is presented for the first time; it is a new thing.[247]

Though the detail is new, the core of the emotion is not new. For, according to Bradley, reproduction is always of universals, and this is true of emotion as well as of ideas. And it is the type, a universal, which is reproduced. There is thus a partial identity between the actual emotion and its artistic reproduction; the universal appears in a new context, reparticularized. Yet what is reproduced as universal is not the old feeling itself, but only its ideal aspect—the content, not the fact. Thus the actual emotion now felt by the reader is nothing he experienced before, but is now for the first time experienced. The <u>particularized universal</u>, says Bradley,

> works directly on the soul, and by that working causes an actual feeling which is like the original. Thus the old feeling, *as* feeling, is in no sense reinstated; but the real fact is that the soul is such . . . that, without restoration . . . and by nothing at all but simple reaction, it responds to the idea with an outcome of feeling . . . . The feeling is not the conclusion of an inference, but . . . mere psychical effect.[248]

Compare Eliot:

> But what we experience as readers is never exactly what the poet experienced, nor would there be any point in its being, though certainly it has some relation to the poet's experience. What the poet experienced is not poetry but poetic material; the writing of the poetry is a fresh "experience" for him, and the reading of it, by the author or anyone else, is another thing still.

Again:

> We have to communicate—if it is communication, for the word may beg the question—an experience which is not an experience in the ordinary sense, for it may only exist, formed out of many personal experiences ordered in some way which may be very different from the way of valuation of practical life, in the expression of it. *If* poetry is a form of "communication", yet that which is to be communicated is the poem itself, and only incidentally the experience and the thought which have gone into it. The poem's existence is somewhere between the writer and the reader; it has a reality which is not simply the reality of what the writer is trying to "express", or of his experience of writing it, or of the experience of the reader or of the writer as reader. Consequently the problem of what a poem "means" is a good deal more difficult than it at first appears.[249]

According to Bradley, the special feelings which, as translated, are combined with the emotion persist as feelings, so that they appear under two different forms at the same time. The poet, accordingly, is able to feel whether the two forms jar or agree. In that way he knows whether the description or representation of the emotion satisfies him and is true. So with the reader. In reading a description of anger or in seeing anger represented in drama, he knows somehow, if versed in such matters, whether the representation is right and true or whether it imports elements alien or false to the emotion in question. What happens here, says Bradley, is that the representation "excites feelings which tend to fill themselves out to the content of the usual felt state. And between this content and

the description offered there is then experienced . . .
the sense of agreement or jar."[250]

The notion of intensity goes with that of the com-
binatory nature of poetry. Eliot says:

> If you compare several representative passages of the
> greatest poetry you see how great is the variety of types of
> combination, and also how completely any semi-ethical
> criterion of "sublimity" misses the mark. For it is not
> the "greatness," the intensity, of the emotions, the com-
> ponents, but the intensity of the artistic process, the
> pressure, so to speak, under which the fusion takes place,
> that counts.[251]

Intensity is substituted for "any semi-ethical criterion
of 'sublimity.' " The word "any" will apply to Longinus, to Kant, and, in particular, to Matthew Arnold.

> Arnold's insistence upon order in poetry according to
> a moral valuation was, for better or worse, of the first
> importance for his age. When he is not at his best he
> obviously falls between two stools. Just as his poetry is
> too reflective, too ruminative, to rise ever to the first
> rank, so also is his criticism. He is not, on the one hand,
> quite a pure enough poet to have the sudden illumina-
> tions which we find in the criticism of Wordsworth,
> Coleridge and Keats; and on the other hand he lacked
> the mental discipline, the passion for exactness in the
> us of words and for consistency and continuity of reason-
> ing, which distinguishes the philosopher. He sometimes
> confuses words and meanings: neither as poet nor as
> philosopher should he have been satisfied with such an
> utterance as that "poetry is at bottom a criticism of life".

A more profound insight into poetry and a more exact
use of language than Arnold's are required. The critical
method of Arnold, the assumptions of Arnold, remained
valid for the rest of his century. In quite diverse developments, it is the criticism of Arnold that sets the tone:
Walter Pater, Arthur Symons, Addington Symonds, Leslie
Stephen, F. W. H. Meyers, George Saintsbury—all the
more eminent critical names of the time bear witness
to it.[252]

And the twentieth century, Eliot has observed, is still
the nineteenth.

Arnold stands for the type of man of letters and
humanist; he stands for "literature" as distinguished
from pure poetry and pure philosophy—in short, he
stands for rhetoric and moralism. This is the tradition
of Cicero, Horace, and Longinus rather than Aristotle, of the Renaissance, which construed Aristotle in
terms of Horace and Latin literature. In this tradition,
poetry is regarded as didactic, and is assessed for its
moral edification. Poetry and prose are not, as Eliot
thinks they should be, sharply distinguished.

Eliot, like Arnold, is offering a concept of order in
poetry; but it is order not according to a moral, but
according to a spiritual, valuation.

It may be observed that the notion of intensity
enters into Bradley's account of morality and religion.[253] Experience, with Bradley, is an incessant
process in which there are distinctions but no divisions,
and a unity at the beginning and the end. The process
of self-realization, which is moral, exists only when
the affirmation of the self in relation to the ideal or
universal will attains a certain strength. In religion
the strength of affirmation—the intensity of feeling as

modified by thought—must be greater than in morality. And the difference is relative, on one side, to the difference in the object. On the other side, the private, morality is conditioned by all kinds of circumstantial matters. Yet morality, poetry, and religion are differentiated.

The combination of "feelings" and "emotions" is infinitely various; and, whatever the combination, the criterion of the poetry is the intensity of the process of combination. As to the effect of poetry, Eliot has this to say:

> The experience of a poem is the experience both of a moment and of a lifetime. It is very much like our intenser experiences of other human beings. There is a first, or an early moment which is unique, of shock and surprise, even of terror (*Ego dominus tuus*); a moment which can never be forgotten, but which is never repeated integrally; and yet which would become destitute of significance if it did not survive in a larger whole of experience; which survives inside a deeper and a calmer feeling.[254]

Here is one form:

> What puts the last cantos of *Don Juan* at the head of Byron's works is, I think, that the subject matter gave him at last an adequate object for a genuine emotion. The emotion is hatred of hypocrisy; and if it was reinforced by more personal and petty feelings, the feelings of the man who as a boy had known the humiliation of shabby lodgings with an eccentric mother, . . . this mixture of the origin of his attitude towards English society only gives it greater intensity.[255]

The general though definite emotion "hatred for hypocrisy" is reinforced by "feelings" originating in boyhood, and the combination constitutes poetry in virtue of its intensity. It may also be observed that Byron's personal and private feelings are here transmuted into the general and universal.

Dryden's poetry offers another form. Of Dryden, Eliot observes that people think he is prosaic because they mistake the material of poetry, the feelings, for the result of the poetic process. The measure of *"poetic ability"* is what one makes of his material. Dryden "makes his object great, in a way contrary to expectation; and the total effect is due to the transformation of the ridiculous into poetry."

> A fiery soul, which working out its way,
> Fretted the pigmy body to decay:
> And o'er informed the tenement of clay.

> These lines are not merely a magnificent tribute. They create the object which they contemplate. Dryden is, in fact, much nearer to the master of comic creation than to Pope. As in Jonson, the effect is far from laughter; the comic is the material, the result is poetry.[256]

Dryden, however, had a commonplace mind; he lacked the insight and profundity to give his poetry the power of suggestiveness.

Marvell penetrates deeper.

> So weeps the wounded balsam; so
> The holy frankincense doth flow;
> The brotherless Heliades
> Melt in such amber tears as these.

These verses have the suggestiveness of true poetry; . . . and we are inclined to infer that the suggestiveness is the aura around a bright clear centre . . . . Marvell takes a slight affair, the feeling of a girl for her pet, and gives it a connexion with that inexhaustible and terrible nebula of emotion which surrounds all our exact and practical passions and mingles with them. Again, Marvell does this in a poem which, because of its formal pastoral machinery, may appear a trifling object:

> Clorinda. Near this, a fountain's liquid bell
> Tinkles within the concave shell.
> Damon. Might a soul bathe there and be clean,
> Or slake its drought?

where we find that a metaphor has suddenly rapt us to the image of spiritual purgation.[257]

With Dante we are as far as we can go. In the episode of Brunetto Latini (Canto XV)

> Poi si rivolse, e parve di coloro
> che coronno a Verona il drappo verde
> per la campagna; e parve di costoro
> quegli che vince e non colui che perde.

> Then he turned, and seemed like one of those who
> run for the green cloth at Verona through the
> open field; and of them he seemed like him who
> wins, and not like him who loses.

One does not need to know anything about the race for the roll of green cloth, to be *hit* by these lines; and in making Brunetto, so fallen, *run like the winner*, a quality is given to the punishment which belongs only to the greatest poetry.[258]

The quatrain, Eliot says, "gives an image, a feeling attaching to an image, which 'came,' which did not develop simply out of what precedes."[259] The image is a particular fact; the feeling attaching to the image is the content of the image, and as such a universal. The relation is that of universal to particular. The image very likely came from Dante's visual experience of the race, though it would make no difference if he had only heard or read about it. It comes in to cap the quatrain with the feeling attaching to a condemned man behaving like a victor, a feeling, we may suppose, which formed the content of Dante's perception, real or imaginary, of proud men condemned—the whole creating the effect of shock and surprise.

So Ulysses, unseen in the hornèd wave of flame,

> Lo maggior corno della fiamma antica
>   cominciò a crollarsi mormorando,
>   pur come quella cui vento affatica.
> Indi la cima qua e là menando,
>   come fosse la lingua che parlasse,
>   gittò voce di fuori e disse: "Quando
> me diparti' da Circe, che sottrasse
>   me più d'un anno la presso a Gaeta . . . . "

The greater horn of the ancient flame began to shake itself murmuring, like a flame struggling against the wind. Then moving to and fro the peak, as though it were the tongue that spoke, threw forth a voice and said: "When I left Circe, who kept me more than a year there near Gaeta . . . ."

is a creature of the pure poetic imagination, apprehensible apart from place and time and the scheme of the poem.[260]

Eliot finds poetry, or something very near to it, not only in verse, but also in prose. Thus in the prose of Lancelot Andrewes the poetry lies in the "relevant intensity."

> When Andrewes begins his sermon, from beginning to end you are sure that he is wholly in his subject, unaware of anything else, that his emotion grows as he penetrates more deeply into his subject, that he is finally "alone with the Alone," with the mystery which he is seeking to grasp more and more firmly. One is reminded of the words of Arnold about the preaching of Newman. Andrewes's emotion is purely contemplative; it is not personal, it is wholly evoked by the object of contemplation, to which it is adequate; his emotions wholly contained in and explained by its object.[261]

With Donne it is different: "Donne is a 'personality' in a sense in which Andrewes is not; his sermons, one feels, are a 'means of self-expression.'"

The process of combining feelings and emotions under pressure—combination and intensity—is the essence of Eliot's poetic theory. It provides him with a criterion which in his hands has led to a revolution of taste in English poetry. Moreover, the qualities he analyzes in terms of this theory are not mere literary qualities or mere personal qualities of the poets who display them; they are the qualities of "a civilization." They imply "a constant inspection and criticism of experience." They may be described as "wit," or "intelligence," or "wisdom." They evince a grasp of human values, "cynical perhaps but untired," leading toward and completed by "the religious conscious-ness."[262]

The theory involves two criteria, one for poetry and the other for the greatness of poetry. Dryden's distinction, for example, is not his greatness, but his poetic ability—his talent for turning the prosaic into the poetic. He works a conjunction of feelings in such a way as to produce surprise. The criterion of great-ness, however, implies a distinction between the per-manent and the transitory.[263]

The business of the poet, according to Eliot, is to use ordinary emotions, and, in working them up into poetry, "to express feelings which are not in actual emotions at all."[264]

Eliot takes exception to Wordsworth's "emotion recollected in tranquillity" because, for one thing, it does not make clear the difference between the emo-tion of art and the emotion of actual life. And of Coleridge Eliot remarks that he fails to do justice to the part that memory plays in imagination, and, in particular, to the importance of what is "instinctive and unconscious" in a poet's selection of "an image, a phrase, a word."[265] In *The Use of Poetry*, in which these criticisms are made, he offers a description of the "auditory imagination":

> the feeling for syllable and rhythm, penetrating far below the conscious levels of thought and feeling, invigorating every word; sinking to the most primitive and forgotten, returning to the origin and bringing something back, seeking the beginning and the end. It works through meanings, certainly, or not without meanings in the ordinary sense, and fuses the old and obliterated and the

trite, the current, and the new and surprising, the most ancient and the most civilised mentality.[266]

The feelings which are not in actual emotions at all may originate in depths below the conscious levels of thought and feeling.

Though Eliot finds Wordsworth's formula for poetry inexact, he says that "in the matter of mimesis he is more deeply Aristotelian than some who have aimed at following Aristotle more closely." "Here," says Eliot, about to quote Wordsworth, "is the new version of Imitation, and I think that it is the best so far: 'Aristotle, I have been told, has said, that Poetry is the most philosophic of all writing: it is so: its object is truth, not individual and local, but general, and operative.' "[267]

In "Poetry and Drama" Eliot offers a still newer version of Aristotle's mimesis:

It seems to me that beyond the nameable, classifiable emotions and motives of our conscious life when directed towards action—the part of life which prose drama is wholly adequate to express—there is a fringe of indefinite extent, of feeling which we can only detect, so to speak, out of the corner of the eye and can never completely focus; of feeling of which we are only aware in a kind of temporary detachment from action . . . . This peculiar range of sensibility can be expressed by dramatic poetry, at its moments of greatest intensity. At such moments, we touch the border of those feelings which only music can express . . . . I have before my eyes a kind of mirage of the perfection of verse drama, which would be a design of human action and of words, such as to present at once the two aspects of dramatic and of musical order.[268]

The problem of drama, which has interested Eliot throughout his career, presents itself to him in terms of feelings and emotions—art and history. The problem is how to work in the feelings which are not in actual emotions, feelings which are indefinite and unfocused, which lie below the level of conscious life.

The transitory and the permanent are associated by Eliot with the conscious and the unconscious. The poetic process is partly unconscious—"a concentration which does not happen consciously or deliberately." And the unconscious lies at the base of the "auditory imagination." It lies also at the base of culture and religion. In *Notes towards the Definition of Culture*, these two, culture and religion, are said to be aspects of a unity and also contrasted and opposed things. Culture as the arts and sciences is only the more conscious part of the unconscious spring of both religion and culture.

> The identity of religion and culture remains on the unconscious level, upon which we have superimposed a conscious structure wherein religion and culture are contrasted and can be opposed. The *meaning* of the terms "religion" and "culture" is of course altered between these two levels. To the unconscious level we constantly tend to revert, as we find consciousness an excessive burden; . . . . We escape from this strain by attempting to revert to an identity of religion and culture which prevailed at a more primitive stage; . . . . [269]

The unconscious with Eliot does not refer to depth psychology, Freudian or Jungian. His general attitude towards psychology makes that plain. Psychology with Eliot as with Bradley and Kant treats of phenomena, the psychic fact as history, and beyond that it has nothing to say. Eliot's citation from Jung in "The Frontiers of Criticism" is, as he intimates, merely a convenience serving the purpose of a popular lecture. It is relevant, however, to the matter under discussion. The point of the quotation, as applied by Eliot, is that poetry can be explained in terms of both external and final causes, and that both are necessary. Though Eliot is there concerned with final causes, there is still the question of the origin of poetry "below the conscious levels of thought and feeling."

With Bradley, the basis of existence is a center of feeling lying below discursive thought. There is no analyzing below this center; and, in one sense, there is no transcending it, for it persists as the basis of all further experience, an inexhaustible reservoir. Bradley, in effect, identifies experience with feeling; and he distinguishes between feeling and consciousness. Feeling is awareness below the level of thought. Consciousness is a development from the feeling center. It arises when some object is brought before the mind; it involves an ideal content, the being of an object for a subject. In short, feeling (though awareness) is, to start with, unconscious, and at all later stages there remains a surplus of such unconscious feeling.[270]

Further, everything that proceeds from the finite center is an ideal construction based on present feeling and perception—and perception includes internal as well as external perception. This is true of our present actual world of space and time, of past and future, and of the worlds we call imaginary. All these worlds, for Bradley, are distinguishable aspects of the one reality, and they all rest ultimately on the single basis of self-feeling. There are, then, various worlds—of art, philosophy, religion, natural science—with relative degrees of reality and value. What Bradley calls "floating ideas" (Eliot speaks of "floating feelings") are ideas which, though unattached to our actual world, may be attached to any one of several other worlds.[271]

My impression is that Eliot in his poetry sticks to experience in the Bradleyan sense. At the same time, when we get to the "bottom," we must assume that we are not expected to find merely a feeling self or the Absolute which is immanent in it, but a reality of another kind. If this is not so, Eliot, we should have to say, "falls apart."

Eliot's "Impersonal" theory of poetry is a theory of poetry as transcendence. There is for him an element in poetry—in experience—which is incapable of elucidation by reference to external causes and conditions.

The history of poetry and criticism, according to him, is only in part a history of flux. Poetry is, to be sure, as various as the human spirit, the manifestations of which in any age are limited and local; and change is constant. Though no one theory will do, a survey of theories need not come to "the stultifying conclusion that there is nothing to be said but that opinion changes." The study of criticism may help us draw some conclusions "as to what is permanent or eternal in poetry, and what is merely the expression of the spirit of an age; and by discovering what does change,

why think ?

and how, and why, we may become able to apprehend what does not change."[272]

As is well known, Eliot's poetry—especially *Four Quartets*—renders a better account than does his criticism of that element in experience which, though incapable of adequate formulation, is eternal amid the flux. It is that reality, in Eliot's phrasing, which is apprehended in the sudden illumination, the moment in and out of time, and which alone redeems the stretch of time. It is there in the memory, in a shaft of sunlight, in the whisper of running streams, in the winter lightning, in the waterfall, in music heard so deeply it is not heard at all; it is here, now, always.[273]

In Eliot's view, the best use of poetry in our time—and the most important use of it in times past—is its concern not with the transient aspects of life, but with those which transcend the dimension of time, though of necessity experienced in time.

For Eliot, the poet is a man speaking to other men. He starts with his own emotions, his personal and private experiences, and is occupied with the struggle to transmute these into something universal and impersonal. Poetry, unlike practical action, is not self-assertion, not the expression of animal feelings. That is what the poet starts with, his material, individual self—his "personality." The end of the poetic impulse is the making of a poem, which is a new thing, quite distinct from the psychological history of the poet. The experience for the poet has the character of a liberation from the burden of practical desire and anxiety (in this sense it is an escape from "personality").[274] The concentration of experiences which constitutes the poem does not happen consciously or deliberately, though the management of the experiences is conscious and deliberate. The concentration or intensity is the consequence of a motion in the poet's soul, a rhythmic stir, penetrating below the conscious levels of thought and feeling, bringing to birth and invigorating word, phrase, and image. These last are directly expressive of the feeling or state of mind which is the inner unity of the poem—that is, its rhythmic stir.[275] They have, however, still another function in the poem. In addition to serving as the vehicle of feeling which animates the poem, words and images are also signs or symbols, and hence necessarily vehicles of meaning in the ordinary sense. A large part of such ordinary meaning may be said to belong to prose. Further, the meaning may be explicit or implicit, determined or undetermined. So far as the meaning is not abstract, but concrete and particular, its associations are theoretically inexhaustible. Still, the pattern of meaning, however rich and however inseparable from the rhythmic stir, plays a secondary part in the poem. The chief use of the meaning in the kind of poetry Eliot is concerned with may be to help divert the reader's mind while the rhythmic stir does its work on him. The meaning, it may be said, stands to the rhythmic stir as the order of practical life stands to the spiritual order. That part of the poem which is incapable of being paraphrased, the rhythmic stir, has a meaning of its own, which, like an outburst of song, points in a direction where words fail though meanings still exist. That is as far as the poetry, as poetry, can go.[276]

It is little wonder, then, that Eliot should say that "the problem of what a poem 'means' is a good deal more difficult than at first appears." Indeed, as he suggests, the poem may mean whatever the reader wishes it to mean (including the reader who does not understand the language) ; for where words fail, each reader is left to the interpretation of his own feelings. The poem leaves the reader in a state of contemplation and silence. It suggests a transcendent order of reality without offering any knowledge of such an order; for poetry is not metaphysics, nor is it mystical vision. It offers some intuition, some feeling, some vision, which is characterized by the absence of practical desire, by the self-forgetfulness of contemplation, and by a unique tranquility.

Eliot knows there is not just one kind of poetry, or just one use of it. Still, it is a knowledge he habitually subordinates to his main critical interests, which are directed by his religious perspective. His readaptation of criticism to a concept of order in poetry according to a spiritual valuation supersedes, for him, the Aristotelian view of poetry, the neo-classic, the Romantic, and the Victorian. It is a modernized version of the scholastic view; and it is this view that underlies his reinterpretation of the tradition of Western poetry.

Eliot does not hold with the doctrine of art for art's sake,[277] either in its *fin de siècle* version or in that of certain contemporary formal critics. The doctrine, he thinks, is largely illusory; and when seriously entertained, a hopeless admission of irresponsibility (he ascribes the doctrine to an extension of Arnold's formula for poetry as a substitute for philosophy and religion). The attempt to find in poetry a "pure" enjoyment, in the sense of separating it from everything else in the world, tends to evacuate it of all significance. One cannot, he believes, rightly understand the poetry of a writer by isolating it from his extra-literary purposes and beliefs. These last do not, indeed, determine the quality of poetry as poetry, but do determine its greatness. What Eliot requires is that a critic know when he is talking about poetry and when about something which is implicated in the poetry or suggested by it.[278]

The principle surely is a sound one, though its soundness does not depend on Eliot's application of it. I do not mean to suggest that Eliot does not apply his own principle. No one perhaps is more expert than he at analyzing the materials that go into poetry and the management of them, and, when he wishes, at separating the materials from their manipulation. But his literary judgments are not confined to technique; and when he is engaged in pronouncing on the importance of poets, his criteria are not strictly literary ones. It must be said that when he departs from his principle, he is aware of what he is doing, and commonly lets his reader know what he is up to. Still, when, as in his pieces on Milton, he acknowledges his bias, the bias is nonetheless at work.[279]

If, as Eliot sees it, poetry is regarded as the verbal equivalent of states of mind or feeling, these two sides of poetry are, for the purposes of criticism, interchangeable. The feeling or states of mind may then be discussed in terms of verbal expression—diction, syntax, rhythm, image. And the qualities on both sides of the equation must be judged by criteria more general than those specific to poetry. The criteria Eliot applies to poetry derive from his religious perspective, as adjusted to the conditions of modern life. And these criteria represent what Eliot understands by tradition.

The perpetuation of tradition in our time, according to Eliot, is not simply a matter of maintaining certain dogmatic beliefs. Nor is there any return to the external conditions of the past associated with such beliefs. Not everything interwoven with such beliefs is essential to them. The vital and the real must be disengaged from the superficial and the sentimental. Further, the tradition of such beliefs must be conceived as a living principle which is capable of diverse historical realizations. It is to be understood not as a fixed and immovable standard, but as a current which discards what is dead and integrates what is alive in the developing mind of Europe.[280] In short, the poet, and the critic, who would be traditional must acquire the "historical sense"—the feeling that the literature of Europe and within it the literature of his own country has a "simultaneous existence and composes a simultaneous order."

The technical aspect of poetry is here related to the notion of poetry as an ideal order—to the permanent and the universal. With Eliot the term "universal" does not carry the sense it has in Aristotle's *Poetics*. In fact, in Eliot's view, Aristotle, owing to his position in time, was not confronted with the problem of what is universal and what was necessary for his time, though, as Eliot expresses it, he did hit on "some of the universals."[281] The universal, Eliot implies, is one thing for a pagan Aristotle and another for a critic living in our time. Nor does the term bear quite the sense it has in the *Critique of Judgment*, or the sense

Wordsworth gives to it in his Preface, though, as has been noted, Eliot believes Wordsworth's interpretation of it is the best up to that time. In the *Poetics*, the term has a moral connotation, referring to the realm of human destiny—that is, the practical order of life. In Kant's *Critique* and in Wordsworth's Preface, though the meaning is again moral, morality is understood in a more inward way than it is by Aristotle. And finally there is Bradley's doctrine of emotions as universals. Thus, according to Eliot, the term "universal" may be variously understood. Aesthetically, it signifies transmuting any permanent impulse into artistic form. So Eliot can speak, without invidious comparison, of both Dante and Shakespeare as universal poets. Metaphysically, it refers to the spiritual order—the order of transcendental or immaterial realities. So Eliot views human impulse and struggle, the horror and the glory of life, in the light of religion. For him, the ultimate meaning of poetry is symbolic in the theological sense.

The field for criticism, then, is the body of literature conceived as an ideal order, and the critic's tools are analysis and comparison. The significance of a poet is determined by his relation to other poets, later and earlier, in the ideal order. One poet is compared with another, not according to the canons of the past or yet those of the present, but according to canons which are, in some sense, universal. The merit of a poet is decided by the degree to which he exemplifies states of mind which evince an awareness of the universal in the temporal. Such an undertaking requires considerable delicacy and tact. For one thing, the determination of status in respect to the main current of tradition is not to be made on the basis of a poet's ideas or moral attitudes in abstraction from his poetry. Eliot's one sustained essay in such abstract criticism, *After Strange Gods,* has not been reissued. No, the determination of status is to be made on aesthetic grounds, by and through the poetry, the generalizations supported by technical analysis, and the whole interlarded with quotations. And the notion upon which it rests is that poetry is, or ought to be, the verbal equivalent of feelings or states of mind, of experience —the "objective correlative."

What Eliot sees in the history of English poetry is "the splitting up of personality."[282] The outlines of the theory are well known. The split, which occurs in the seventeenth century, marks a break in the tradition of English poetry. The causes of the split, which must be sought in Europe as well as in England, lie at a depth at which words and concepts fail us. The alteration in poetic language and the Civil War in England are both consequences of the same ineffable causes. The main line of the tradition, which is characterized by a unified personality, is represented on the continent by Dante and other poets of his school; and in England by Shakespeare, the later Elizabethan dramatists, and the early Jacobean poets (in France it appears eminently in Racine and Baudelaire).

The difference, Eliot says, between these poets and those coming after the Civil War is not a mere difference in degree; it reflects a change in the mind of Europe. The "mechanism of sensibility" has altered, and so, too, have the poetic uses of language. The metaphysical poets, for example, possess, in varying degrees, the ability to respond directly to the com-

plexity of experience—physical, moral, and intellectual—and to recreate it in language which is faithful
to its concrete texture. Thereafter the English mind
loses the capacity for direct and unified response to
life. A secondary, and inferior, tradition begins with
Milton (and a subordinate tradition with Dryden).
The feeling in poetry is now cruder than it was: it is
less complicated, subtle, and various; it is not now the
precise equivalent of the impressions of sense and the
play of mind. As a consequence of this dissociation,
it shortly degenerates into sentimentality: the thought or
sense, no longer controlling the feeling, grows vague and
abstract. And the language becomes conventional. Poets
feel and think by fits and starts, unbalanced; or they
turn poetry into a vehicle for expressing ideas. With
some exceptions—Blake, perhaps Wordsworth, Keats,
La Forgue, Corbière, and Baudelaire—poetry turns outward, as it were, disregarding the realities of the soul.

Eliot's demonstration proceeds by analysis and comparison of one poet with another within the ideal order
of poetry. It is, for the most part, an analysis of the poetry of details rather than the poetry of design. In Eliot's
theory of poetry, both these aspects spring from the
same root in the soul of the poet. All poetry, of whatever kind, represents the transformation of personal
emotion into an external form. The emotion, as embodied in the poem, is of a different kind and quality
from its origin in the personal experience of the poet—
it is an artistic emotion, in virtue of its form. The
emotion which informs the poem is what the poem is
in itself—the entelechy of the poem. That emotion, according to Eliot, informs not only the verse, but also
the agents and the action.[283] So far as a poem or poetic

drama is of uniform inspiration, the poetry may be illustrated by a phrase, a verse, an agent, or the design of the whole.

Again, the essence of the poem being its informing emotion, the rhythm is of the first importance. Since emotion and rhythm are intimately related, the quality of the rhythm indicates something of the quality of the emotion. Rhythm or emotion varies according to strength, intensity, balance, subtlety, and variety. Since emotion does not exist in isolation, but points to objects and thoughts, its quality can be indicated only by its relation to these. Thus the emotion in a poem will be vague or precise according to whether its reference to objects and thoughts is less or more explicit and according to the number and quality of objects and thoughts. Such references—meanings—do not, it will be recalled, exist for themselves; their primary function in the poem is to define the emotion which is the *esse* of the poem. Moreover, the objects, say, which are present in the poem by virtue of its words and images, are themselves symbolic of meanings which lie beyond words and concepts—meanings which are "here, now, always." As for the imagery in a poem, it will be better or worse—more or less poetic—depending on its power to suggest or evoke feelings which point beyond objects and concepts.

The effect of such poetic power is a shock of surprise, of joy, of sudden illumination. We are for the moment beside ourselves, rapt in the intuition of a reality. Here "literature" has become "poetry." The poet has used his "medium" not to express his personal feelings or opinions, but to make present realities which spring from feelings, deep and obscure, lying below the level of intellect. And here poetry as art or technique no longer counts, for it "leads toward, and is only completed by, the religious comprehension." And this is the function of poetry, the sense in which it may be said to provide "consolation"— "strange consolation, which is provided equally by writers so different as Dante and Shakespeare."[284]

A poetics of this kind allows a person with Eliot's skill the greatest flexibility in the criticism of literature and life. It allows him to take a thing in its literal sense only or in its symbolic sense or in both senses together. He can, and does, move nimbly from technical analysis to moral commentary to philosophic generalization to symbolic interpretation. He is able to make a distinction between literature and life and at the same time to conceive them as mutually illuminating. The theory can be applied at any level: to distinguish the "literary" from the "artistic"; poetry and drama which, though good of its kind, is of the surface from that which has a strong inner significance; rhythms which display a crude sensibility from those which display a refined one; imagery which is functional and evocative from that which is distractive and rhetorical; syntax which is faithful to the workings of mind and feeling from that which is a simplification of experience.

It is a poetics, finally, which assumes that the significance of life is not exhausted by the satisfactions and frustrations of practical activity, with its related emotions, or even by the pleasures of the intellect. For Eliot, the general utility of poetry is that it offers not only aesthetic pleasure, but also such consolation as can be found in the obscure intuition of transcendental reality.

CHAPTER **9**

AESTHETICS
AND HISTORY

WHOEVER TAKES UP THE subject of criticism nowadays finds that all lines lead to Eliot (and I. A. Richards), as once they led to Arnold and, to go no further, Wordsworth and Coleridge. Considered in itself, Eliot's criticism is certainly an achievement of the first order. It is the same mind, working in much the same way, in both the poetry and the criticism. And the criticism is, of course, the best commentary on the poetry. It was written in the main as an explanation and defense of the kind of poetry he was striving to write. That it finds its justification in his poetry will, I assume, be agreed.

It is another matter, however, to take his criticism apart from his poetry, and from his general beliefs, and to substitute it for the tradition of humane studies.

Eliot's criticism has a negative as well as a constructive side. His negations, as has been said, derive partly from his aesthetic point of view, and, it must now be added, partly from his religious point of view. In general, Eliot's objection to the criticism of the last two centuries or so is that it is motivated by a secular scheme of valuation. During this time, owing to the decay in religion and the alterations in political institutions, poetry, he says, assumed new functions, and criticism adjusted itself to these changes. The result is that both the poetry and the criticism are inextricably involved with the general values of this period. Though the basis of its values is secular, its criticism, Eliot holds, is nevertheless preoccupied with the problem of religion, in the sense that it seeks in literature a substitute for values which are properly the concern of religion. He is, accordingly, opposed to virtually every version of education—Richards' as well as Arnold's—which finds in literature a moral or edifying element. He does not deny that moral criteria are applicable to literature—he is not an exponent of art for art's sake—but, in his view, a morality divorced from its religious background is little more than mindless custom and habit.[285]

According to Eliot, literature may be "substantive" —self-contained—only so far as there is in any age common agreement on matters of ethics and theology.[286] But such agreement has not obtained since the close of the Middle Ages. With the Renaissance, when poetry was gradually dissevered from philosophy and religion, the humanities, Eliot thinks, have rested on nothing but common sense; and literature has in-

creasingly become the stay of those who have lost
their intellectual convictions and religious faith. Eliot
consistently decries the modern critics and educators
who, following the Romantics and the Victorians,
find in literature some equivalent of, or substitute
for, moral, philosophic, and religious values.
And one main object of his criticism has been
to distinguish poetry from these several disciplines.
Partly he is arguing here for the aesthetic point of
view. Yet, unlike some other critics who also urge
such a view, Eliot is not content with a merely negative
idea of poetry. His position on this matter comes to
this: poetry may be employed to teach extra-literary
values, but such values do not depend on the poetry
as poetry, nor is the poetry a substitute for such values.

The chief object of Eliot's negations has been the
uses to which literature has commonly been put in
secular education. When he is dealing with this point
—the educator's view of poetry—his prose invariably
grows crabbed and captious. His practice then is to
dismiss poetry as mere entertainment; or to allow it
the higher status of aesthetic pleasure; or, acknowledg-
ing it as a serious activity, to define it as an enigmatical
emotional experience. At such times, nothing will explain poetry—not communication, or history, or psychology, or mythology, or mysticism. Indeed, in this
mood, Eliot will not consent to the validity of any
form of interpretation. And the reason doubtless is
that, in a world dominated by secular values, no form
of interpretation is likely to be quite satisfactory in
spirit and perspective. If a critic fixes on the right
poem, he is likely to appreciate it for the wrong
reason; or he will ignore a poet's ideas when these are

integral to his poetry, or discover ideas in a poem which is empty of them. In any event, his secular bias is bound to lead him into one kind of error or another. Hence a popular audience, with no learned prejudices, is preferable to an audience of the half-educated or the ill-educated. There is the poetry, and there is the reader with his sensibility; and the only valid meaning of the poetry is the reader's interpretation of his feelings when he reads the poetry.

Eliot's criticism, in effect, removes literature, with its variety of purposes, from its historical framework and places it ultimately in a theological perspective. It does not, to be sure, ignore the conditions of time and place—what Eliot calls sociological criticism—but it transcends them. The individuality of the poet and his historical circumstances are merely the conditions of poetry, the materials with which every poet must work. The business of the poet is to turn his private experiences and the thought of his time into poetry. In so doing, he will, in greater or lesser measure, make his poetry an expression of his age. But the part of his poetry which is universal, and hence most important, is not explicable by reference to his personal life or historical conditions. Nor can it be adequately defined in intellectual terms.[287] Its significance is emotional in the spiritual, not the practical, sense. Its object is not to produce in the reader emotions of a practical kind, but to release him from such emotions. Its effect, it may be said, is a scholastic version of Aristotle's catharsis. It is not

simply the pleasure of an emotional relief, together with the perception of what is universal in human destiny; rather, the release from the burden of practical life has the character of contemplation which is suggestive of transcendental reality.

If, then, what is most important in poetry is inexplicable by reference to the life of the poet and historical circumstances; and, if apart from technical matters, this is what "criticism" is concerned with, it follows that scholarship is subordinated to "criticism." And with the subordination of scholarship goes that of history, for scholarship corresponds to history in its most general sense. And with the subordination of these goes that of the humane culture of which they are the chief instruments. This relation of "criticism" to history and scholarship—to humane studies—has been a basic position with Eliot from the start. It is given expression not only in his prose, but also in his poetry.

> . . . There is, it seems to us,
> At best, only a limited value
> In the knowledge derived from experience.
> The Knowledge imposes a pattern, and falsifies,
> For the pattern is new in every moment
> And every moment is a new and shocking
> Valuation of all we have been.

Eliot, to be sure, recognizes the rights of scholarship, though he takes a rather narrow view of scholarly activity. He thinks scholarship is concerned with fact, and "criticism" with the use of it. With this restriction, he believes scholarship is serviceable to those who know how to employ or ignore its facts. The scholar, as he represents him, is commonly engaged in fact-collecting as an end in itself, and hence busy with the satisfaction of some extra-literary interest.

Still, the scholar may serve a useful if humble service. His facts not only guard us against the outright misunderstanding of a text, but also prepare us for understanding it. The task of the literary scholar as such, it would appear, is to present a selection of facts which are relevant to a work of literature—its conditions, setting, genesis. At this point, "criticism," as Eliot understands it, takes over.

Surely, this confusion of scholar and pedant is unwarranted, if not wilful. On the other hand, though it has seemed to modern "critics" to offer them a basis for the depreciation of "history," Eliot has directed his harshest strictures not at scholarship, but at the pretentious criticism, in journals and books, which, going beyond the data of a work, supplies opinion or fancy. Facts being neutral, they do not corrupt taste; criticism which employs a text for the propagation of opinion does corrupt it. What Eliot has in mind, besides the retailing of second-hand opinion, is the large part of critical writing which consists of "interpretation." "Instead of insight," he says, "you get a fiction." His general objection to such criticism is that it is based on a misunderstanding of the nature of poetry, and hence of criticism. Indifferent to the aesthetic nature of literary art, it takes poetry as the conscious expression of the opinions of the poet rather than as a process of giving emotion artistic form.[288] The opinions of the poet, Eliot observes, turn out in most cases to be those in which the critic is interested.

This is true enough. But if what Eliot gets out of poetry is not "interpretation," the term is a meaningless counter. Like other "critics," Eliot finds in poetry what he brings with him. His strength is first that, taking language as the verbal equivalent of feelings and states of mind, he can discuss matters of the gravest import in terms of diction, syntax, imagery, and rhythm; and he can do all this while talking apparently about poetry and not another thing. Further, what Eliot brings with him, as critic as well as poet, is not merely his "personality," but tradition. But he brings it in a highly personal form. Indeed, what strikes one in Eliot's view of tradition is the strong personal note. It is as though tradition were important because Eliot is interested in it. And this perhaps is true so far as Eliot's criticism is instrumental to his métier of poet—he connects his derogation of Milton with the kind of poetry he wishes to write. If "personal" is the wrong word, at all events the composition of Eliot's thought is no less individual than Milton's. That is the way of strong poets. And we may leave the last word to Bradley:

> Or he [the individual] may rather have several worlds without rational unity, conjoined merely by co-existence in his own personality. And this separation and disconnectedness (we may fail to observe) is, in some degree, normal.

If we take Eliot's criticism apart from his general beliefs, we are left with the aesthetic point of view. There are literary facts, and there is the critical use of them, the tools of which are analysis and comparison. Facts do not teach their own use, nor do the critic's tools. The critic's guide, it would appear, is his sensibility and taste. Hence criticism, Eliot holds, can never be a science. Criticism by itself is a mere

skill, and a mere means—in Eliot's view the means to
the enjoyment of literature and the education of taste.
The understanding and appreciation of poetry is, as
Aristotle observes in the *Politics,* part of civilized life.
And, in this respect, Eliot's view of the place of poetry
in life is not unlike Aristotle's, though his aesthetics
is of the more generalized modern type. But it is the
aesthetics of a man who has a philosophy and a
dogmatic religion, and it is adjusted to the perspective
of these disciplines.

What Eliot appears to offer is a plan for a literary
education which would be suitable to a seventeenth-
century gentleman who held to the Anglo-Catholic
faith, or to a sensitive and intelligent modern person
of the same or similar faith who would avoid the
secular valuation of life assumed in the academic
study of literature and who would yet cultivate literature as a means of enjoyment and instruction. In the
essay "Religion and Literature" and in the Note on
the development of taste in *The Use of Poetry,* he
suggests how this end may be pursued, the Note on
taste concluding thus:

> This note is really introductory to a large and difficult
> question: whether the attempt to teach students to ap-
> preciate English literature should be made at all; and
> with what restrictions the teaching of English literature
> can rightly be included in any academic curriculum, if
> at all.

Eliot's observations in this connection deserve the
attention of teachers of English—at least of those who

conceive their object to be not the inculcation of opinion, but, to begin with, the training of independent students. I refer to those passages in which Eliot is treating of the effect of literature on the inward person and of the organization of such experiences. He is speaking, in these passages, of the state of excitement which, especially in our younger days and in a more critical form in our later ones, attends our reading of poets: of the introduction to new worlds of experience, of the possession which successive poets take of us, of the outburst of scribbling that frequently results from these seizures, and of the adjustment of such experiences in accordance with our peculiarities of character.

It will be agreed that Eliot's emphasis is exactly placed, for it is in the inward life that literature finally either matters or does not. If literature is to matter, there must be a genuine response on the part of the student, and the organization of such responses must be the result of the self-activity of the student. If what we are speaking of is literary culture, it is a consequence of activities pursued for their own ends and for their own sakes. The organization—the culture—is not directly transferable from teacher to student, assuming that the teacher has it—and, if it were, to attempt to impose it would be a misconception of the teacher's function.

The teacher is a mediator, concerned with method, with means for developing the student's powers of thought and feeling. But method is relative to suppositions about the nature of literature and a humane education, to *theoria*, to the insight which must direct the process. If it is replied that the process must be haphazard, a matter of pure chance, rather than partly amenable to direction and partly not, it may be rejoined that a literary and humane education which is unable to say what it professes to teach *in* what it teaches cannot hope to offer anything more than a means of employment, and will ever tend to be a sophistic art of rhetoric, as Socrates argues with as much reason as may fairly be required of him.

Eliot, in discussing a literary education, supposes nothing more to be required than sensibility and the criteria derived from a definite ethical and religious position. He adopts the notion that scholarship is, more or less, the aimless pursuit of facts—indifferent to the fact of a philosophy of scholarship. So, in altercation with the so-called New Humanists, he subjects the notion of a humane education to the same depreciation as scholarship. His tone of harsh contention, in this altercation, springs from the fact that the exponents of the New Humanism would offer their views as a substitute for religion.

If, as Eliot contends, there is nothing in the idea of a humane education which requires that it be considered in opposition to religion, is it true to say, as Eliot does, that humanism is dependent upon religion? In order to support this proposition, Eliot offers the notion of a "*pure* humanistic attitude"[289]—that is, a humanism detached from its basis in history and dependent upon nothing but sensibility and taste. Religion finds its principles in an act of faith, and a humane education finds its principles in experience and reason. Humanism has been, and may be, subsumed under religion, but its principles do not derive from religion. True, experience and reason have their limitations. Still, we must strive to preserve the humane education which issues from them, for it is the best thing we have—religion, though in this world, is not of it.

Eliot does indeed set the problem which underlies the contemporary controversy about "criticism" and "history." Humanism, he holds, reposes upon nothing but sensibility and common sense. If humanism is but a synonym for general culture, it is true, as Eliot affirms, that its axioms are unformulable. The notion of a general culture, considered by itself, is indefinite, with no specific content. It is a result of study, and not merely of literary study, but of any liberal study which is properly pursued. Historically, the humanities have been associated with the study of the ancient classics, with the life, letters, and thought of Greece and Rome; and in more recent times with the life and thought and feeling of modern nations. The humanities have in all periods been conceived as leading to a general, not merely a literary, culture. The Renaissance humanists, for example, were concerned primarily with ancient culture, and with poetry as a part of that culture. They regarded the body of classical, or secular, studies as forming a unity in itself, calling it variously *litterae*, or *eloquentia*, or *philologia*. "When I say letters," remarks a typical Renaissance humanist, "I mean philosophy which is conjoined with eloquence."[290] To the humanists, philosophy did not mean what Plato calls dialectic, or Aristotle first philosophy, or the scholastics metaphysics (sometimes theology). It meant rather the body of secular learning represented by classical culture; it meant the wisdom embodied in that culture, together with its techniques of expression. In this respect, humanism does not appeal to an intellectual system or a religious one. It appeals to the experience of the past, in particular to the tradition of learning and culture—"the best which has been thought and said."

In all this there is nothing which lends itself to exact formulation. Moreover, "the best which has been thought and said" is subject to constant re-interpretation. Since many now find it in the special modern sciences, physical and social, it appears to them that such sciences are a better medium for "humanism" than the humanities. The idea of a humane education evidently means nothing to numerous persons of unquestioned intelligence. Its very worth is widely repudiated; and the idea of humanity which informs it is, for the most part, unintelligible.

The humane culture of which I have been speaking, however indefinite its content, is not, after all, without an intellectual basis. The humanist Battista Guarino, in a book published in 1459, wrote: "To man only is given the desire to learn. Hence what the Greeks called *paideia* we call *studia humanitatis;* for learning and virtue are peculiar to man; therefore our forefathers called them *'humanitas,'* the pursuits, the activities, proper to mankind."[291] The notion of pursuits proper to mankind suggests a certain view of the nature of man and his status in the world. This Renaissance humanist, whether he knew it or not, was appealing to the notion first elaborated by Plato and after him by his pupil Aristotle that man as man has a function which transcends his special activities, a general function, which is common to all men in virtue of their humanity. The notion is restated by

Kant. And it is this notion, for example, that Wordsworth appeals to when, in the Preface, he speaks of the poet's object as "giving immediate pleasure to a human Being possessed of that information which may be expected from him, not as a lawyer, a physician, a mariner, an astronomer, or a natural philosopher, but as a Man." And if Wordsworth's interpretation of this notion is not exactly that of Plato's or Aristotle's, it is not independent of Greek philosophy.

The ultimate object of literary scholarship is humanistic; its final purpose is to transmit the idea of humanity which is the keystone of Western civilization, together with the humanizing ideas and ideals which derive from it, as progressively enlarged and deepened and diversely applied. There is no historical justification for the arbitrary limitations popularly placed upon scholarship. The concept is represented neither by fact-collecting nor by textual preoccupations, though these are included in it. There is no genuine scholarship, whatever the incidental utility of the work, without critical assimilation of the matters of which it treats, and without the philosophic insight which enables one to rise above the details of his work and relate them to the ultimate purpose of his activity. And scholarship of this kind is indistinguishable from humanism or culture.

The two, scholarship and humanism, cannot in fact be separated without producing the extremes of pedantry and sentimentalism. They are the body and spirit of one organism; and if the body apart from the spirit is lifeless, the spirit apart from the body is bloodless—something less than full humanity. "Criticism" is not an independent discipline; it cannot, therefore, provide an adequate foundation for humane studies. A "criticism" which turns its back on history and scholarship is open to platitude, eccentricity, and pretentiousness. The history of human development, as empirically established, makes possible the valuation of different ages by reference to an ideal of humanity derived from the development of humanity itself.

Footnotes

1. *On Poetry and Poets* (New York: Fararr, Straus and Cudahy, 1957).

2. *The Sacred Wood: Essays on Poetry and Criticism* (New York: Barnes & Noble, Inc., 1928), Preface to the 1928 Edition.

3. *Selected Essays, 1917-1932* (New York: Harcourt, Brace & Co., 1932).

4. *The Use of Poetry and the Use of Criticism: Studies in the Relation of Criticism to Poetry in England* (London: Faber and Faber, Ltd., 1933).

5. *The Sacred Wood*, pp. 11-12.

6. *Ibid.*, p. 32.

7. *Selected Essays*, p. 6.

8. *On Poetry and Poets*, p. 118.

9. *The Use of Poetry*, p. 119.

10. *On Poetry and Poets*, p. 299.

11. *Ibid.*, p. 171.

12. *The Use of Poetry*, p. 35.

13. *Selected Essays*, pp. 295, 303, 305; see also pp. 46-50. **In** *The Use of Poetry* see pp. 121-42.

14. *Selected Essays*, p. 11.

15. "Religion and Literature," *Selected Essays* (New York: Harcourt, Brace and Co., 1950), p. 343.

16. *The Use of Poetry*, p. 143.

17. *Ibid.*, pp. 149-52.

18. Cf. August W. Schlegel: "It belongs to the general philosophic theory of poetry, and the other fine arts, to establish the fundamental laws of the beautiful. Every art, on the other hand, has its own special theory, ... The general theory . . . seeks to analyze that essential faculty of human nature—the sense of the beautiful, which at once calls the fine arts into existence, and accounts for the satisfaction which arises from the contemplation of them; and also points out the relation which subsists between this and all other sentient and cognizant faculties of man. To the man of thought and speculation, therefore, it is of the highest importance, but by itself alone it is quite inadequate to guide and direct the essays and practice of art.

"Now, the history of the fine arts informs us what has been, and the theory teaches what ought to be accomplished by them. But without some intermediate and connecting link, both would remain independent and separate from one and other, and each by itself, inadequate and defective. This connecting link is furnished by criticism, which both elucidates the history of the arts, and makes the theory fruitful." *(Lectures on Dramatic Art and Literature*, trans. John Black [2nd ed., London: George Bell and Sons, 1892], pp. 17-18.)

19. *The Use of Poetry*, pp. 15-30.

20. *The Sacred Wood*, p. 15.

21. Eliot distinguishes between the impulse to create and the impulse to criticize. Criticism is intellectual—analysis and construction. It is involved, or ought to be involved, in creation, where it is instrumental to the creative impulse. But unfulfilled creative impulse often seeks an outlet in criticism. The disturbance of the soul, when it does not lead to creation, works itself out in criticism, and something new is produced which is neither criticism nor creation. Since the poet finds fulfilment of the creative impulse in poetry, his criticism is likely to be free of the irrelevant emotion which distorts the criticism of the unsatisfied, emotional critic.

22. *Selected Essays*, pp. 19-20.

23. *The Sacred Wood*, p. 11.

24. *Ibid.*, pp. 10-11.

25. *Nicomachean Ethics*, Bk. VI.

26. *The Sacred Wood*, p. 10.

27. *Ibid.*, pp. 12-13.

28. *Selected Essays*, p. 20.

29. *The Sacred Wood*, pp. 14-15.

30. *Ibid.*, p. 10.

31. *The Use of Poetry*, pp. 47, 48, 49, 54; *The Sacred Wood*, p. 12.

32. *The Use of Poetry*, pp. 45-46.

33. *Ibid.*, pp. 46-47.

34. *Ibid.*, pp. 42-44.

35. "Shakespearian Criticism: I. From Dryden to Coleridge," in *A Companion to Shakespeare Studies*, ed. H. Granville-Barker and G. B. Harrison (New York: Doubleday & Co., Inc., 1960), pp. 299-301.

36. "Preface to Shakespeare," *Shakespeare Criticism: A Selection*, introd. D. N. Smith (London: Oxford University Press, 1934), p. 98. Cf. Dryden, "An Essay of Dramatic Poesy," *English Critical Essays (16th, 17th, and 18th Centuries)*, ed. E. D. Jones (London: Oxford University Press, 1930), pp. 165-66.

37. "Preface to Shakespeare," p. 99.

38. "Shakespearian Criticism," p. 302.

39. **"An Essay of Dramatic Poesy," pp. 129-30; "Preface to Shakespeare,"** p. 97.

40. *De Vulgari Eloquentia*, Bk. II, chaps. 2-4, 9; "Epistola X." In *A Translation of the Latin Works of Dante Alighieri* (London: J. M. Dent & Sons, Ltd., 1934).

41. "Shakespearian Criticism," pp. 304-5.

42. "Of the Standard of Taste," in *Essays Moral, Political and Literary* (2 vols.; London: Longmans, Green, & Co., 1882), I, 268-69; "An Enquiry Concerning the Principles of Morals," II, 239.

43. "An Enquiry Concerning Human Understanding," *op. cit.*, II, 135.

44. For Baumgarten, see Bernard Bosanquet, *A History of Aesthetic* (London: George Allen & Unwin, Ltd., New York: The Macmillan Co., 1934), pp. 182-87; Ernst Cassirer, *The Philosophy of the Enlightenment*, trans. Fritz C. A. Koelln and James P. Pettegrove (Boston: Beacon Press, 1955), pp. 338-60; E. F. Carritt, ed., *Philosophies of Beauty: From Socrates to Robert Bridges, Being the Sources of Aesthetic Theory* (London: Oxford University Press, 1950), pp. 81-85.

45. Etienne Gilson, expounding Descartes's notion of clear and distinct ideas, says that "it is the nature of ideas to be mutually exclusive in mathematics, each containing everything that comes under its definition, and nothing more." "In short, clearness comes to ideas from the fact that we ascribe to them all that belongs to their nature, distinction comes to

them from the fact that we deny to them all that does not belong to their nature." (*The Unity of Philosophical Experience* [New York: Charles Scribner's Sons, 1952], pp. 153-54, 160.) Leibniz says: "An *obscure* or vague idea is one that does not suffice for the recognition of its object . . . . If I can recognize the thing I have *clear* or vivid knowledge of it, but this again may be either confused [sensuous] or distinct [intellectual]. It is confused if I cannot enumerate one by one the marks which suffice for distinguishing the thing from others . . . . Thus we see painters and other artists well enough aware what is right and what is faulty, but often unable to give any reason for their taste: if asked, they reply that the work they dislike lacks a *je ne sais quoi*." (Carritt, *op. cit.*, p. 57.) Bosanquet says: "I imagine that what is meant by clear and confused through this whole succession of philosophies may be illustrated by the possibility of adequately expressing this or that matter in words. I suppose that a clear idea is one which is so cut down and defined as to be communicable by a conventional sign with a tolerable degree of adequacy, while a confused idea is one which remains of a kind and complexity—such as a harmony of colour—which language cannot reproduce. That the 'confused idea' can have an *order* of its own, which is appreciable to feeling, seems to be presupposed in the idea of beauty, and insisted on by Baumgarten in his discussion." (*Op. cit.*, pp. 183-84.) Cassirer, expounding Leibniz, says: "The procedure of 'distinct knowledge' can then be no other than that of resolving every complex phenomenon into the various elements which determine and condition it. So long as this resolution has not been finished, so long as any unanalyzed complex remains in any of these elements, the real goal of 'adequate' comprehension has not been attained. Our concept is commensurable with its object only when it succeeds not merely in reflecting this object but in causing it to develop before us, in tracing it back to its original elements and in reconstructing it from them." (*Op. cit.*, p. 343.)

46. The idea of perfection plays an important part in the thought of the Leibniz-Wolff-Baumgarten school. According to Leibniz, the existing universe exhibits the highest degree of perfection. Again, Wolff uses the idea to explain beauty: "Beauty consists in the perfection of a thing so far as the thing is apt thereby to produce pleasure in us . . . . [e.g. We call a picture beautiful because of its resemblance to its subject]." (Carritt, *op. cit.*, p. 81.) So Baumgarten: "The appearance of perfection, or perfection obvious to taste in the wide sense, is *beauty;* the corresponding imperfection is ugliness. Hence beauty, as such, delights the observer; ugliness, as such, is disgusting." (Carritt, p. 84.) Of the idea of perfection as entertained by Leibniz (as well as by Descartes and Spinoza) Bosanquet says: "It might be generally defined as the character of a whole in so

far as this whole is affirmed by its parts without counter-action, and thus perfection became a postulate of everything real, because reality depended upon power to harmonize with the greatest number of conditions. In Wolff, therefore, it naturally comes to mean the mere logical relation of the whole to part, or unity in variety, and this is the sense in which Baumgarten also employs it. The content of beauty for him is therefore nothing more than our old friend the formal principle of unity in variety which may, of course, at any moment take the form of teleology. Whatever is opposed to the perfection of sensuous knowledge, that is to the unity of parts in the whole of the sense-percepion, is ugly." (*Op. cit.*, p. 185.)

Baumgarten defines a poem as a "sensuous discourse." A poem is perfect "in proportion as its component parts arouse many sensuous ideas." The poetic quality of sensuous ideas resides in their clearness and vividness; definiteness and complexity of sensuous ideas make for clearness and vividness, and hence for good poetry. Feelings and emotions are eminently poetic, and the stronger they are, the clearer and more vivid is the poetry. Poetic ideas should be ordered and connected in such a way as to constitute a definite and unified impression (Carritt, *op. cit.*, pp. 81-85).

47. Trans. F. Max Müller (2 vols.; London: Macmillan Co., 1881), II, 19.

48. "116. The Greek philosophers and the Fathers of the Church already sufficiently distinguished *aistheta* from *noeta* (objects of thought). But obviously for them *aistheta* were not to be identified with things perceptible by the senses, for objects not actually present, namely imaginations, were so called. *Noeta,* as what can be known by the higher faculty of knowledge, are the object of logic; *aistheta* belong to the aesthetical science or to Aesthetic." (Baumgarten, in Carritt, *op. cit.*, p. 84.)

49. Kant published an essay in 1764 entitled *Observations on the Feeling of the Beautiful and Sublime.* See James Creed Meredith, *Kant's Critique of Aesthetic Judgement,* Translated with Seven Introductory Essays, Notes and Analytical Index (London: Oxford University Press, 1911), essay ii—hereafter cited as Meredith.

50. Cf. Johnson on criticism and science, in W. R. Keast, "The Theoretical Foundations of Johnson's Criticism," *Critics and Criticism: Ancient and Modern,* ed. R. S. Crane (Chicago: University of Chicago Press, 1952), pp. 396-97.

51. The problem in the *Critique of Pure Reason* is: "how are synthetical *a priori* cognitive judgments possible?" The problem in the *Critique of Judgment* is: "how are judgments of taste possible?" Since, according to Kant, judgments of taste are synthetical, the problem of the *Critique of Judgment* "belongs to the general problem of transcendental philosophy: how are synthetical *a priori* judgments possible?" (*Critique of Judgment,*

trans. J. H. Bernard [New York: Hafner Co., 1951], pp. 130-31)—hereafter cited as Bernard.

52. Bernard, pp. 12-15.

53. *Ibid.*, pp. 127-28, *et passim.*

54. The allusion is to the Leibniz-Wolff-Baumgarten school of thought. Kant's quarrel with this school is not confined to its mistaking a logical for an aesthetic judgment; it extends to its taking knowledge of phenomena for knowledge of metaphysical reality. In the *Critique of Pure Reason,* Kant, after explaining that theoretical knowledge is concerned with phenomena, not with non-sensuous reality (the thing-in-itself), says:

"It would vitiate the concept of sensibility and phenomena, and render our whole doctrine useless and empty, if we were to accept the view (of Leibniz and Wolf), that our whole sensibility is really but a confused representation of things, simply containing what belongs to them by themselves, though smothered under an accumulation of signs (Merkmal) and partial concepts, which we do not consciously disentangle. The distinction between confused and well-ordered representation is logical only, and does not touch the contents of our knowledge . . . .

"This shows that the philosophy of Leibniz and Wolf has given a totally wrong direction to all investigations into the nature and origin of our knowledge, by representing the difference between the sensible and the intelligible as logical only. The difference is in truth transcendental. It affects not the form only, as being more or less confused, but the origin and contents; so that by our sensibility we do not know the nature of things by themselves confusedly only, but not at all . . . ." (pp. 38-39.)

Perfection: Kant identifies perfection with the good. Both involve the concept of an objective purpose and the reference of an object to that concept. Whatever satisfies that concept is judged to be good, either good for something, utilitarian, or good in itself, according to its concept. Hence, if beauty is reducible to the concept of perfection, there is no specific difference between aesthetic judgment and the judgment of things as good. The distinction between a confused and a clear thought does not represent a difference of kind, for both involve concepts, and therefore they are logical or cognitive, not aesthetic (Bernard, pp. 62-65).

55. *Ibid.*, pp. 123-27.

56. The critic, as such, does not go to work with a general formula and judge particular works in the light of that formula; his procedure is not syllogistic. His proper job is to analyze in a given form the way in which imagination and understanding work in relation to each other and to the pleasure or displeasure which their working occasions in the critic. Such analysis, Kant says, is psychological, not philosophic. He seems to mean

that it is not the abstract analysis of the mental powers involved in art; it is the elucidation of the empirical details of form as related to the state of mind of the critic (*Ibid.*, pp. 127-28).

Both critics and teachers of the fine arts find it convenient to employ rules and precepts, but these are mere mnemonic aids or maxims the object of which is to lead one to feel the beauty of a work of art and to judge it by feeling (*Ibid.*, pp. 200-201).

Thought and image: What Kant calls "aesthetic ideas" involve thought as well as images. The thought, however, is logically indeterminate. There is an activity of mind behind the imagery, and the imagery stimulates an activity of mind in the reader, and in both cases the activity is indefinite, suggesting more than can be formulated in language (*Ibid.*, pp. 156-63).

Humanities: The reason, in general, is that art is a serious activity of the human spirit, and the humanities are concerned with the diverse cultivation of the spirit (*Ibid.*, pp. 200-202).

57. *Critique of Pure Reason*, pp. 45-46.

58. "It has hardly struck any psychologist that this imagination is a necessary ingredient of perception. This was partly owing to their confining this faculty to reproduction, partly to our belief that the senses do not only give us impressions, but compound them also for us, thus producing pictures of objects. This however, beyond our receptivity of impressions, requires something more, namely, a function for their synthesis." (*Ibid.*, fn., pp. 105-6; see also 101-12.)

Kant's analysis is philosophic, not psychological. When he speaks of imagination, he means the a priori or productive imagination, not the empirical or reproductive one. Both, of course, are necessary for experience. The reproductive imagination has its laws of association, but these presuppose the synthetic activity of the productive imagination. The laws of association explain how experience is constructed, but they do not explain what makes such construction possible and hence necessary.

59. Bernard, p. 25.

60. *Ibid.*, p. 38.

61. A logical judgment may employ concepts of the understanding or ideas of the practical reason. The difference is that in the first instance there is, and in the second there is not, theoretical cognition—the determination of external objects. In the judgment, Metals are bodies, we have knowledge of a sensible object, a definite cognition involving ultimately an intuition of sense as corresponding to the concept of metal. In the judgment, Fraud is deplorable, we have a logical judgment

of the moral reason, but no theoretical cognition, for there is no intuition of sense which corresponds to the idea of fraud.

Kant's use of "cognitive" and "cognition" varies with the context. Sometimes he speaks of any logical judgment—any employment of concepts—as cognitive; at other times he speaks of judgments of the understanding as producing cognitions—theoretical knowledge—and judgments of the reason as non-cognitive (*Ibid.*, pp. 15-17, 25-31, 187-89).

62. *Ibid.*, pp. 8, 54-55.

63. *Ibid.*, p. 31; see also Part II, "Critique of the Teleological Judgment."

By assuming that the world of sensible objects is a whole composed of parts adjusted to the idea of the whole, as though it were conceived by a basic intellignce, we obtain a principle which regulates our investigation of the mechanism of nature, and thus extends our theoretical knowledge. Again, by assuming that the same basic intelligence conceived the world in such a way that happiness is the outcome of behavior as determined by the laws of practical reason, we obtain a principle which regulates our moral reasoning and renders intelligible our expectations of felicity. Apart from the notion of purpose—of the adaptation of means to ends—we should not be able to explain these matters to ourselves.

Kant starts with the will as the "cause which acts in accordance with concepts." By abstracting from the will, he gets the notion of a concept as the cause of an effect. This is objective purpose, which always involves concepts. It is one kind of purpose without purpose (the will). Then, by abstracting the form of an object from its concept, and coupling the form with feeling, he arrives at the essential aesthetic fact. This is formal or subjective purpose, which is another instance of purpose without purpose.

64. *Ibid.*, p. 58.

65. *Ibid.*, pp. 38-45, 46-48, 58-65, *et passim.*

66. Hume, in "A Dissertation of the Passions":

"1. Some objects produce immediately an agreeable sensation, by the original structure of our organs, and are thence denominated Good; as others, from their immediate disagreeable sensation, acquire the appellation of Evil. Thus moderate warmth is agreeable and good; excessive heat painful and evil.

"Some objects again, by being naturally conformable or contrary to passion, excite an agreeable or painful sensation; and are thence called *Good* or *Evil*. The punishment of an adversary, by gratifying revenge, is good; the sickness of a companion, by affecting friendship, is evil.

"2. All good or evil, whence-ever it arises, produces various passions and affections, according to the light in which it is surveyed.

"When good is certain or very probable, it produces Joy: When evil is in the same situation, there arises Grief or Sorrow.

"When either good or evil is uncertain it gives rise to Fear or Hope, according to the degree of uncertainty on one side or the other.

"Desire arises from good considered simply; and Aversion, from evil. The Will exerts itself, when either the presence of the good or absence of the evil may be attained by any action of the mind or body."

Hume goes on to distinguish between the objects and the causes of passions. The objects are the self and other persons; and the causes, though infinitely various, are the sensations of pleasure and pain. For the rest, the mind is a series of changes based on "'the double relation of sentiments and ideas," according to the principles of resemblance, contiguity, and causality.

Kant seems to accept Hume's empirical psychology so far as it goes, but with him psychological analysis does not go far enough; and his transcendental point of view leads to an elaboration and refinement of distinctions.

He objects, for one thing, to Hume's reducing all satisfactions—those of sense, of the good, and of beauty—to sensations of pleasure and pain. The effect of this procedure is to set up utility as the sole judge of value. To avoid the confusion created by this usage, Kant makes a distinction between "sensation" and "feeling." "Sensation" is external: it is the perception of an object of sense—the green of a meadow; "feeling" is internal, the pleasure that attaches to the perception. With Kant, then, "sensation" is objective, as referring to external objects; and what is external carries with it, directly or indirectly, an "interest": the relation of desire to an object, actual or possible. "Feeling," on the other hand, is subjective. It may refer to an object of sense, or to a concept of the good, or to bare form. The pleasant is what gratifies the sense; the good is what is approved by the reason; and beauty is independent of both sense and reason. One difficulty is that Kant uses "sensation" to designate both external and internal sensation, perception and feeling (Bernard, pp. 39-41).

Kant distinguishes between physical pleasure and intellectual or moral pleasure. If the pleasure precedes an act of thought, which involves concepts, it is physical. It is based on sensation, which is passive. Physical, too, are the combinations of sensations, the internal tensions, the moving forces, which we call emotion. The organization of the body, together with sensation and emotion, constitutes the physical order of things. The moral order is constituted by reason and by the feeling which is the effect of reason, the pleasure or pain we take in the agreement or disagreement of action with the moral law.

Kant also distinguishes "emotions" from "passions." "Emotions" are related to "feeling," the subjective state which precedes reflection. "Emotions" are states of mental excitement, blind, impulsive, and transient—for example, resentment which flares and subsides. "Passions" are related to desire, the will, and hence have objective reference. "Emotions" are states of excitement which, so to speak, lie below the will or desire. "Emotions," we may say, are merely subjective, whereas "passions" are objective (*Kant's Critique of Practical Reason and Other Works on the Theory of Ethics*, trans. Thomas Kingsmill Abbott [6th ed.; London: Longmans, Green & Co., Ltd., 1927], pp. 265-68, 289, 310, 319-20).

"Emotions" are of two kinds, "spirited" and "tender." The propensity to the latter is called "sentimentality." The examples Kant gives suggest the passive indulgence of emotion: inconsolable or imaginary grief; romances and pathetic plays; shallow moral precepts and religious discourse which fails to inculcate resolution and self-reliance. Though "emotions" precede reflection, and indeed are obstacles to it, they may be combined with ideas. Kant gives as examples "emotion" combined with religious and social ideas. These are perhaps "emotions" of the "spirited" kind. They are not to be confused, however, with moral feeling, which does not precede, but follows, reflection (Bernard, pp. 112-15).

In the "Analytic of the Beautiful," Kant says:

"*Emotion*, that is a sensation in which pleasantness is produced by means of a momentary checking and a consequent more powerful outflow of the vital force, does not belong at all to beauty. But sublimity [with which the feeling of emotion is bound up] requires a different standard of judgment from that which is at the foundation of taste; and thus a pure judgment of taste has for its determining ground neither charm nor emotion—in a word, no sensation as the material of the aesthetical judgment." (*Ibid.*, p. 62.)

The sublime: The feeling of the sublime is a state of mind occasioned by the magnitude or power of physical objects—the stars, a turbulent sea, and the like. The imagination is unable, say, to comprehend the stars in "a whole of intuition," and the mind falls back on reason, which can think the totality of the stars. Totality is a supersensible idea, for no intuition of sense corresponds to it; it is also an absolute measure, by comparison with which every sensible measure is small. Thus the incapacity of imagination leads to the consciousness of the superiority of reason, the faculty of the supersensible and the source of moral ideas. The feeling of the sublime is thus the consciousness that the moral nature of man exceeds the reach of sense and imagination. Again, confronted by an object of nature, a turbulent sea, whose power is irresistable, we suffer the pain of our physical limitations; but again we find relief in the consciousness of a faculty which exceeds and is independent of everything physical. Man as an object makes a poor showing in relation to the power of physical nature. The sublime is a state of mind in which one becomes aware that the true standard of greatness is moral, not physical; that the worth of humanity, which resides in the moral spirit, surpasses the worth of everything physical; and that whatever pertains to the physical existence of man—goods, health, life—is of little account as compared to the obligation to fulfil the destiny of man, which is a free life according to the moral law. It is the idea of humanity that preserves man from submission to the power of natural forces, within and without; apart from this idea, the immensity and power of physical forces inspires only terror and superstition.

Beauty and the sublime are both aesthetic judgments. The object in both is referred to feeling; and the judgment is "disinterested"—unconditioned by sensation or concept. With beauty, however, the feeling is attached to the contemplation of form, whereas with the sublime it is attached to the sphere of the supersensible, the moral sphere.

Since moral (intellectual) good involves interest, it would seem that the good was incompatible with a pure aesthetic judgment. But, if the good is presented as sublime, that is, aesthetically, no conflict occurs. Moral purpose involves desire mediated by reason. Reason, by itself, is a pure intellectual satisfaction, whereas desire represents the "interest" of the physical man. If moral good is exhibited in such a way that the "interest" of sense and emotion is denied and sacrificed, reason, as a pure intellectual satisfaction, is left; then, by referring reason to feeling, we get an aesthetic judgment in which abstraction is made from all "interest."

There can be no aesthetic judgment of the sublime if one is in actual danger or feels actual fear. Contemplating a great waterfall, one simply imagines its power and one's inability to cope with it. The impression is purely imaginative: it is the result of the immediate intuition of the waterfall and whatever feelings are thereby evoked. In other words, one abstracts from sensation and concept. If the waterfall is used to generate electricity, the aesthetic judgment disregards this purpose, as well as any physical discomfort occasioned by the spray and the uproar of the water. The judgment attends only to the impression excited by a tremendous mass of water in turbulent descent.

In a drama, the representation of moral character—action determined by moral principles or ideals, action indifferent to personal well-being— is sublime or aesthetic. Thus courage and nobility are aesthetically sublime emotions; they arouse in us the consciousness of the greatness of humanity

(*Ibid.*, pp. 68-118). A general, Kant says, is aesthetically more satisfying than a statesman—and thereby hangs many a political tale.

67. "Whatever by means of reason pleases through the mere concept is good." The satisfaction here is the effect of an intellectual (moral) judgment. The good always involves a concept of objective purpose and the reference of an object to that concept. The agreement of the object with the concept is the good. If the purpose is external to the object, the good is utilitarian; if internal, it is perfection. Thus far we have been dealing with purpose apart from will. When we put in the will, we are dealing with moral action, with ethics. Since the will is defined as desire mediated by reason, the good here, virtue, is the agreement of an action with the moral law. In both cases, with or without the will, the good is determined by reason; and the pleasure attached to the determination of the good may be denominated a moral or an intellectual satisfaction. The feeling which is the effect of a judgment of the good is moral feeling (*Ibid.*, p. 41).

68. *Critique of Pure Reason*, p. 13.

69. Bernard, pp. 119-20.

70. *Ibid.*, secs. 9, 37. These are the key sections. See, in general, "Deduction of Pure Aesthetical Judgments," beginning with sec. 30.

71. *Ibid.*, secs. 18, 19, 20, 21, 22, 40.

72. *Ibid.*, p. 44.

73. A theoretical judgment does not involve a conscious feeling of pleasure or pain. It is only reflective judgments that do this, judgments according to subjective or objective purpose, aesthetic or moral judgments (*Ibid.*, pp. 24, 46).

74. The mind, according to Kant, is a unity of powers which are severally autonomous and independent, each with its proper a priori principle. Kant provides the following table:

List of Mental Faculties	Cognitive Faculties
Cognitive faculties	Understanding
Feeling of pleasure and pain	Judgment
Faculty of desire	Reason
A priori Principles	Application
Conformity to Law	Nature
Purposiveness	Art
Final purposes	Freedom

(*Ibid.*, pp. 32-34).

75. *Ibid.*, pp. 127-28.

76. *Ibid.*, pp. 77, 129.

77. For the schematization of concepts, see *Critique of Pure Reason,* II, 121 ff.

78. "The understanding alone gives the law." And the conformity of imagination is *"to law of the understanding* in general (Bernard, p. 78)." In *Critique of Pure Reason* (p. 133), Kant says of the principle of contradiction: "It is a general though only negative criterion of all truth, and belongs to logic only, without reference to its object, and simply declares that such contradictions would entirely destroy and annihilate it." Cf. Alfred North Whitehead on propositions and imaginative feeling. The relevant part concerns the "suspense-form" of entertaining a "datum." The "datum" is neither "identical, nor incompatible" with the object of "contrast." Very much simplified, the point is that artistic "propositions" need not agree, but must not be incompatible, with fact *(Process and Reality: An Essay in Cosmology* [Reprint; New York, 1941], p. 413; see pp. 281, 395-405, 412-28). Again, Whitehead, speaking of "the method of rigid empiricism," induction, says: "What Bacon omitted was the play of a free imagination, controlled by the requirements of coherence and logic." *(Ibid.,* p. 7.) The difference between the "imaginative thought" of philosophy and poetry is one of method.

79. "There are indeed in general two ways *(modi)* in which . . . a man may put together his notions of expressing himself; the one is called a *manner (modus aestheticus),* the other a *method (modus logicus).* They differ in this that the former has no other standard than the *feeling* of unity in the presentment, but the latter follows definite *principles;* hence the former alone avails for beautiful art." (Bernard, p. 162.)

"Thus we can readily learn all that Newton has set forth in his immortal work on the *Principles of Natural Philosophy,* however great a head was required to discover it, but we cannot learn to write spirited poetry . . . . The reason is that Newton could make all his steps, from the first elements of geometry to his own great and profound discoveries, intuitively plain and definite as regards consequence, not only to himself but to everyone else. But a Homer or a Wieland cannot show how his ideas, so rich in fancy and yet so full of thought, come together in his head, simply because he does not know and therefore cannot teach others. In science, then, the greatest discoverer only differs in degree from his laborious imitator and pupil, but he differs specifically from him whom nature has gifted for beautiful art. And in this there is no depreciation of those great men to whom the human race owes so much gratitude, as compared with nature's favorites in respect of the talent for beautiful art. For in the fact that the former talent is directed to the ever advancing greater perfection of knowledge and every advantage depending on it, and at the same time to the imparting this same knowledge to others—in this it has a great superiority over [the talent of] those who deserve the honor of being called geniuses. For art stands still at a certain point; a boundary is set to it beyond which it cannot go, which presumably has been reached long ago and cannot be extended further. Again, artistic skill cannot be communicated; it is imparted to every artist immediately by the hand of nature; and so it dies with him, until nature endows another in the same way, so that he only needs an example in order to put in operation in a similar fashion the talent of which he is conscious." (*Ibid.*, pp. 151-52.)

Kant does not mean that artists can afford to be indifferent to technical requirements or negligent of the labor necessary for the mastery of technique; nor is "inspiration" a substitute for hard thought. Kant has little patience with "shallow heads" who "believe that they cannot better show themselves to be full-blown geniuses than by throwing off the constraint of all rules," or with a public which naively mistakes unintelligibility for profundity of thought (*Ibid.*, p. 153).

80. *Ibid.*, pp. 155-56.

81. *Ibid.*, pp. 148, 149, 161.

It is also the feeling *of* the free play of the cognitive faculties, a feeling which manifests itself as a sense of vitality. So it might be said, as Wordsworth and Coleridge say, that the poet takes pleasure in the vital motions of his spirit or soul, and this in spite of the hard work of writing verse.

82. *Ibid.*, p. 157.

83. "In the most universal signification of the word, ideas are representations referred to an object, according to a certain (subjective or objective) principle, but so that they can never become a cognition of it. They are either referred to an intuition, according to a merely subjective principle of the mutual harmony of the cognitive powers (the imagination and the understanding), and they are then called *aesthetical;* or they are referred to a concept according to an objective principle, although they can never furnish a cognition of the object, and are called *rational ideas.* In the latter case the concept is a *transcendent* one, which is different from a concept of the understanding, to which an adequately corresponding experience can always be supplied and which therefore is called *immanent.*

"An *aesthetical idea* cannot become a cognition because it is an *intuition* (of the imagination) for which an adequate concept can never be found. A *rational idea* can never become a cognition because it involves a concept (of the supersensible) corresponding to which an intuition can never be given." (*Ibid.*, p. 187.)

84. *Ibid.*, pp. 157-58.

85. *Ibid.*, p. 158.

86. *Loc. cit.*

87. *Ibid.,* pp. 158-59.

88. *Ibid.,* p. 159.

89. *Ibid.,* pp. 159-60.

90. *Ibid.,* p. 160.

91. " . . . a product composed with soul and taste may be given the general name of poetry." (Kant, as quoted by Meredith, *op. cit.,* essay iv, p. lxxxv; *Anthropology, Werke,* vol. vii, p. 246.) Cf. A. W. Schlegel: "Poetry, taken in its widest acceptation, as the power of creating what is beautiful, and representing it to the eye or the ear, is a universal gift of Heaven, being shared to a certain extent even by those whom we call barbarians and savages." (*Op. cit.,* pp. 18-19.) Cf. Wordsworth's discussion, in the Preface, of Johnson's stanza "I put my hat upon my head, etc." This trivial matter, Wordsworth says, "is neither interesting in itself, nor can *lead* to anything interesting; the images neither originate in that sane state of feeling which arises out of thought, nor can excite thought or feeling in the Reader." In short, it wants "soul."

Of music Kant says: "Its charm . . . appears to rest on this that every expression of speech has in its context a tone appropriate to the sense. This tone indicates more or less an affection of the speaker and produces it also in the hearer, which affection excites in its turn in the hearer the idea that is expressed in speech by the tone in question. Thus as modulation is, as it were, a universal language of sensations intelligible to every man, the art of tone employs it by itself alone in its full force, viz. as a language of the affections, and thus communicates universally according to the laws of association the aesthetical ideas naturally combined therewith. Now these aesthetical ideas are not concepts or determinate thoughts. Hence the form of the composition of these sensations (harmony and melody) only serves instead of the form of language, by means of their proportionate accordance, to express the aesthetical idea of a connected whole of an unspeakable wealth of thought, corresponding to a certain theme which produces the dominating affection in the piece." (Bernard, pp. 172-73.)

92. "The mental powers, therefore, whose union (in a certain relation) constitutes genius are imagination and understanding. In the employment of the imagination for cognition, it submits to the constraint of the understanding and is subject to the limitation of being conformable to the concept of the latter. On the contrary, in an aesthetical point of view it is free to furnish unsought, over and above that agreement with a concept, abundance of undeveloped material for the understanding, to which the understanding paid no regard in its concept but which it applies, though not objectively for cognition, yet subjectively to quicken the cognitive powers and therefore also indirectly to cognitions. Thus genius properly

consists in the happy relation [between these faculties], which no science can teach and no industry can learn, by which ideas are found for a given concept; and, on the other hand, we thus find for these ideas the expression by means of which the subjective state of mind brought about by them, as an accompaniment of the concept, can be communicated to others. The latter talent is, properly speaking, what is called spirit; for to express the ineffable element in the state of mind implied by a certain representation and to make it universally communicable—whether the expression be in speech or painting or statuary—this requires a faculty of seizing the quickly passing play of imagination and of unifying it in a concept (which is even on that account original and discloses a new rule that could not have been inferred from any preceding principles or examples) that can be communicated without any constraint [of rules]." (*Ibid.*, pp. 160-61.)

93. *Ibid.*, pp. 155-56, 162-63. Genius is the animating principle of the mind, the autonomy of soul or spirit, the vitality of thought and feeling. It is an original element in the constitution of things which is incapable of logical determination. But we are all familiar with its exemplary character. A person writing prose, say, runs out of power; his genius has for the time being abandoned him. For want of something better to do, he picks up a book and begins reading. It often happens that, if the book is written with soul or spirit, it ignites the animating principle of the reader's mind, and he is ready to write again. If prose or verse is not exemplary, it is dead, written without soul or spirit. But inspiration is a fact. Spirit re-creates itself directly in those with the gift for receiving it.

Cf. Meredith: "Human nature, the whole heritage of the race, descends upon the man of genius, and he receives it into himself, not so as to over-power his individuality, but so as to give his individuality force and truth." (Essay vi, p. cxxxv.)

Cf. Eliot: "I can recall clearly enough the moment when, at the age of fourteen or so, I happened to pick up a copy of Fitzgerald's *Omar* which was lying about, and the almost overwhelming introduction to a new world of feeling which this poem was the occasion of giving me. It was like a sudden conversion; the world appeared anew, painted with bright, delicious and painful colours. Thereupon I took the usual adolescent course with Byron, Shelley, Keats, Rossetti, Swinburne." (*The Use of Poetry*, p. 33.) Again, still speaking of the period of youth: "The frequent result is an outburst of scribbling which we may call imitation, so long as we are aware of the meaning of the word 'imitation' which we employ. It is not deliberate choice of a poet to mimic, but writing under a kind of daemonic possession by one poet." (*Ibid.*, p. 34.) Again: "A very young man, who is himself stirred to write, is not primarily critical or even widely appreciative. He is looking for masters who will elicit his consciousness of what he wants to say himself, of the kind of poetry that is in him to write. The taste of an adolescent writer is intense, but narrow: it is determined by personal needs. The kind of poetry that I needed, to teach me the use of my own voice, did not exist in English at all; it was only to be found in French. For this reason the poetry of the young Yeats hardly existed for me until after my enthusiasm had been won by the poetry of the older Yeats; and by that time—I mean from 1919 on—my own course of evolution was already determined." (*On Poetry and Poets,* pp. 295-96.)

94. Cf. Meredith, essay vi, pp. cxxi-cxxvi.

95. Bernard, pp. 133-35.

96. *Ibid.,* pp. 170, 172.

97. *Ibid.,* p. 161.

98. *Ibid.,* p. 165.

99. *Ibid.,* p. 141.

100. " . . . Aesthetic sensibility involves the revelation of no mystery of nature: it involves no deep insight into the hidden meaning of things— whatever the *Critique of Taste* may disclose in respect of our own nature. In adopting this position Kant was well advised. The realm of feeling extends over the broad and dusky demesnes of a twilight consciousness. It is in this realm that poetry has its *immediate* truth. But the inspiration of poetry has a higher *source*. Poetry looks back upon that realm and returns to it. It is only one who has looked out towards ideas of reason that can re-enter into the twilight, and there allow his dreams to take mystic shape in its half-seen forms. . . . The originality of the man of genius (in the case of fine art) consists in his capacity for detaching *himself* from feeling, which he then possesses as his empire." (Meredith, essay vii, pp. clv-clvi.)

101. Bernard, secs. 64, 65, 66, 76, 77, 83, 84, all in Part II, "Critique of the Teleological Judgment."

102. *Ibid.,* pp. 116, 190.

103. *Ibid.,* p. 186.

104. *Ibid.,* p. 119.

105. *Ibid.,* pp. 184-87, 192.

106. *Ibid.,* p. 189.

107. "The merit of Art in its service to civilization lies in its artificiality and its finiteness. It exhibits for consciousness a finite fragment of human effort achieving its own perfection within its own limits. Thus the mere toil for the slavish purpose of prolonging life for more toil or for mere

bodily gratification, is transformed into the conscious realization of a self-contained end, timeless within time. The work of Art is a fragment of nature with the mark on it of a finite creative effort, so that it stands alone, an individual thing detailed from the vague infinity of its background. Thus Art heightens the sense of humanity. It gives an elation of feeling which is supernatural. A sunset is glorious, but it dwarfs humanity and belongs to the general flow of nature. A million sunsets will not spur on men towards civilization. It requires Art to evoke into consciousness the finite perfections which lie ready for human achievement." (A. N. Whitehead, *Adventures of Ideas* [New York: Macmillan Co., 1933], p. 348.)

108. Eliot's impersonal theory of poetry appears to many persons as thin and cold—"too intellectual." Eliot, I think, takes note of this view when he says: "There are many people who appreciate the expression of sincere emotion in verse, and there is a smaller number of people who can appreciate technical excellence. But very few know when there is an expression of *significant* emotion, emotion which has its life in the poem and not in the history of the poet. The emotion of art is impersonal. And the poet cannot reach this impersonality without surrendering himself wholly to the work to be done." (*Selected Essays,* p. 11.) Again: "For the great majority of people who love poetry, 'religious poetry' is a variety of *minor* poetry: the religious poet is not a poet who is treating the whole subject matter of poetry in a religious spirit, but a poet who is dealing with a confined part of this subject matter: who is leaving out what men consider their major passions, and thereby confessing his ignorance of them." ("Religion and Literature," *op. cit.,* p. 345.)

Kant takes note of a similar objection to the sublime: "We need not fear that the feeling of the sublime will lose by so abstract a mode of presentation—which is quite negative in respect of what is sensible—for the imagination, although it finds nothing beyond the sensible to which it can attach itself, yet feels itself unbounded by this removal of its limitations; and thus that very abstraction is a presentation of the Infinite, which can be nothing but a mere negative presentation, but which yet expands the soul. Perhaps there is no sublimer passage in the Jewish law than the command, 'Thou shalt not make to thyself any graven image, nor the likeness of anything which is in heaven or in the earth or under the earth,' etc. This command alone can explain the enthusiasm that the Jewish people in their moral period felt for their religion, when they compared themselves with other people, or explain the pride which Mohammedanism inspires. The same is true of the moral law and of the tendency to morality in us. It is quite erroneous to fear that, if we deprive this [tendency] of all that can recommend it to sense, it will only involve a cold, lifeless assent and no moving force or emotion. It is quite the other way; for where the senses see nothing more before them, and the unmistakable and indelible idea of morality remains, it would be rather necessary to moderate the impetus of an unbounded imagination, to prevent it from rising to enthusiasm, than through fear of the powerlessness of these ideas to seek aid for them in images and childish ritual. Thus governments have willingly allowed religion to be abundantly provided with the latter accompaniments, and seeking thereby to relieve their subjects of trouble, they have also sought to deprive them of the faculty of extending their spiritual powers beyond the limits that are arbitrarily assigned to them and by means of which they can be the more easily treated as mere passive beings." (Bernard, p. 115.)

109. *Ibid.*, pp. 196-200.

110. *Ibid.*, pp. 70, 285-86.

111. *Ibid.*, p. 139.

112. *Ibid.*, pp. 218-19.

113. *Ibid.*, pp. 201-2.

114. *Ibid.*, p. 139.

115. We have conversation and music with our food, write and read poetry based on sex, adorn our clothes, and hang paintings on the walls of our dwellings and in public galleries, and in Europe there are the churches and the cathedrals. Art transforms the animal basis of life. For the "aesthetics" of Italy see Henry James's *Italian Hours*.

116. *Ibid.*, p. 140.

117. *Ibid.*, p. 282.

118. *Ibid.*, p. 201.

119. Though the ground of aesthetic judgment is neither social nor intellectual, taste may be joined indirectly with both. The question is whether the intellectual interest in the past is not more vital to aesthetic appreciation than modern critics seem to think. Consider, for example, the question of the authenticity of works of art. Does it make no difference who created a work of art, Michelangelo or an unknown apprentice, Shakespeare or Bacon? The concern is not mere curiosity about a name; it is an interest in the existence of a particular intelligible spirit. To be sure, art is not defined by truth, in the intellectual sense, but it must not be incompatible with the general criteria of truth. Though indirect, the relation of truth to art is of great importance, not as a constitutive, but as a regulative, element. So the study of art which is indifferent to the scientific element of art cannot long sustain interest.

120. "After the initial basis of a rational life, with a civilized language, has been laid, all productive thought has proceeded either by the poetic insight of artists, or by the imaginative elaboration of schemes of thought

capable of utilization as logical premises. In some measure or other, progress is always a transcendence of what is obvious." (A. N. Whitehead, *Process and Reality*, p. 14.)

121. Bernard, e.g., p. 105.

122. Roughly, Homer, by virtue of his genius, gained something for mankind, but it was not until the establishment of a stable culture that the Greeks began to take a conscious aesthetic interest in his poems. Plato judged them by moral and intellectual criteria. Aristotle advanced the notion that poetry has its own standard of fitness and is to be judged primarily by its own laws. Yet Aristotle's *Poetics* presupposes an audience of moral culture. Tragedy, according to Aristotle, does not teach moral ideas; the pleasure it affords presupposes such ideas.

123. Bernard, p. 136.

124. But cf. Meredith, essay vi, p. cxxiv.

125. Bernard, p. 149.

126. *Ibid.*, pp. 136-37.

127. This is Whitehead's phrase. See *Process and Reality*, p. 23; *Adventures of Ideas*, pp. 30-31, *et passim*. "The Greek philosopher who laid the foundation of all our finer thoughts ended his most marvelous dialogue with the reflection that the ideal state could never arrive till philosophers are kings. Today, in an age of democracy, the kings are the plain citizens pursuing their various avocations. There can be no successful democratic society till general education conveys a philosophic outlook." (*Adventures of Ideas*, pp. 124-25.)

128. Bernard, pp. 138, 160, 171.

129. *Ibid.*, p. 170.

130. *Ibid.*, p. 67.

131. *Ibid.*, pp. 147-48.

John Crowe Ransom is, as he has told us, a Kantian. See, e.g., "New Poets and Old Muses," *American Poetry at Mid-Century* (The Library of Congress, 1958). Section 49 of Kant's *Critique*—the exposition of aesthetic ideas—is, I think, the basis of Ransom's poetic theory of "logical structure" and "superfluity" of "texture," the "prose object" and "the tissue or totality of connotation." So, in "Criticism, Inc.," he says: "Behind appreciation, which is private, and criticism, which is public and negotiable, and represents the last stage of English studies, is historical scholarship. It is indispensable. But it is instrumental and cannot be the end itself. In this respect historical studies have the same standing as linguistic studies: language and history are aids." (*The World's Body*, p. 339.)

132. *Critique of Pure Reason*, pp. 10-11.

133. Eliot on Kant: "True, he [Bradley] was influenced by Kant and Hegel and Lotze. But Kant and Hegel and Lotze are not so despicable as some enthusiastic mediaevalists would have us believe, and they are, in comparison with the school of Bentham, catholic and civilized and universal (*Selected Essays*, p. 362)." "In spite of all the hard (and just) things Mr. Babbitt and Mr. More have said about Kant, the second generation of humanism seems to found its ethics on a similar basis to Kant's (*Ibid.*, p. 396)." In *The Use of Poetry*, after remarking that Richards "on his own showing, is engaged in a rear-guard religious action," he adds a footnote: "Somewhat in the spirit of 'religion without revelation', of which a greater exponent than Mr. Julian Huxley was Emmanuel Kant. On Kant's attempt (which deeply influenced later German theology) see an illuminating passage in A. E. Taylor's *The Faith of a Moralist*, vol. ii, chap. ii (p. 135)."

Kant's concept of faculties of the mind which are relative to distinct orders of experience is not unlike that of Aristotle and Aquinas. With Kant, however, the world is not independent of the mind; it is rather partly the creation of the mind. Post-Kantian philosophers of idealism go beyond Kant in their notion of the Absolute as the unifying principle of experience. The Absolute differs from the analogous principle in Aristotle and scholasticism in being immanent in, not external to, the self and the world. The Absolute is, so to speak, refracted by the self, and appears as poetry, religion, and philosophy, all three being regarded as aspects of the same truth, though differing in their manner of specifying it.

134. *On Poetry and Poets,* pp. 9-10.

135. *Ibid.,* p. 12.

136. *The Sacred Wood,* pp. viii-x.

137. *The Use of Poetry,* pp. 22-23, *et passim.*

138. *Ibid.,* p. 15.

139. *Selected Essays,* pp. 19, 13.

140. *On Poetry and Poets,* p. 117.

141. *Selected Essays,* p. 267.

142. "Religion and Literature," *op. cit.,* p. 343.

According to J. C. Ransom and R. Wellek, this position disqualifies Eliot from full membership in the society of new critics. Ransom, in *The New Criticism,* admires and trusts Eliot's poetic instinct as operative in his criticism, but questions his competence as a theorist of poetry. Eliot, he says, is a half-hearted aesthetician. Though he talks about poetry as autotelic and discusses poetic effects, he sees a poem, for the most part, in the light of other comparable poems. The relation he seeks to establish is the degree of conformity of a poet's practice to the "tradition" of English and European poetry; and such judgments are not aesthetic, but historical.

Ransom, accordingly, denominates Eliot not a new, but a historical, critic. Eliot, he observes, in the matter of historical scholarship is "a Pharisee of the Pharisees." To be sure, the use he makes of his learning, Ransom says, sets him apart from academic literary scholars; for, unlike these last, he employs his learning for the sake of literary understanding after the fashion of such scholarly critics as Dryden and Johnson. But such an approach to literature, Ransom remarks, is after all what one would expect our departments of English to foster, though their actual concern is with extra-literary matters. "And," he concludes, "if Eliot is one of the most important sources of a new criticism, it is because here the new criticism is in part the recovery of old criticism." (p. 140.)

Ransom if anyone should know whether a critic is a new critic or not. In *The New Criticism* (p. 3), he says that "most critical writing is done in the light of 'critical theory,' which unfortunately is something less than aesthetics." In "Criticism, Inc.," he says: "Criticism is the attempt to define and enjoy the aesthetic or characteristic values of literature." A new critic, Ransom seems to say, is or should be a strictly aesthetic or philosophic critic, and few of the so-called new critics satisfy this definition.

In *Theory of Literature*, R. Wellek and A. Warren also identify criticism with aesthetics; and, though their aesthetics differs from Ransom's, they, too, find that Eliot does not quite make the grade of new critic, for the reason that in evaluating literature he employs extra-aesthetic as well as aesthetic criteria (pp. 253-57).

143. *Selected Essays*, p. 368.

In the Preface to his work on logic, Bradley says: "I fear that, to avoid misunderstandings, I must say something as to what is called 'Hegelianism.' For Hegel himself, assuredly I think him a great philosopher; but I never could have called myself an Hegelian, partly because I can not say that I have mastered his system, and partly because I could not accept what seems his main principle, or at least part of that principle. I have no wish to conceal how much I owe to his writings; but I will leave it to those who can judge better than myself, to fix the limits within which I have followed him. And for the 'Hegelian School' which exists in our reviews, I know no one who has met with it anywhere else." (*The Principles of Logic*, 2nd ed., revised with commentary and terminal essays [2 vols.; London: Oxford University Press, 1950], p. x.)

144. "Religion and Literature," *op. cit.*, pp. 345, 346.

145. In "Dante," Eliot says: "Furthermore, we can make a distinction between what Dante believes as a poet and what he believed as a man." Such a distinction, he implies, is relative to the purity of the poetry. The purer the poet, the more his private beliefs are transformed in becoming poetry, the more he creates a world which stands apart from the poet as

man. Purer here seems to mean impersonal or objective. With Dante, though not with Goethe, there is, to begin with, a coherent system of accepted ideas and morals, which, since it is not the private work of the poet, stands apart from him "for understanding and assent even without belief." There was thus less need or temptation for Dante than for Goethe as well as other modern poets to use his poetry for the expression of his private views, and the appreciation of his poetry, accordingly, is less involved with his private views than is that of modern poets. As for the Catholic system itself in its relation to Dante's poetry, we need regard it only as we would any other coherent system of thought (*Selected Essays*, p. 219).

146. *The Use of Poetry*, p. 113.

147. See Maurice De Wulf, *An Introduction to Scholastic Philosophy, Medieval and Modern (Scholasticism Old and New)*, trans. P. Coffey (New York: Dover Publications, Inc., 1956).

148. See, e.g., Bk. II, Part I, *The Principles of Logic*.

149. Perhaps the most convenient statement of Bradley's doctrine of experience is given in "On Our Knowledge of Immediate Experience," chap. vi, in *Essays on Truth and Reality* (London: Oxford University Press, 1914)—hereafter cited as *Essays*. See also "Thought and Reality," chap. xv, in *Appearance and Reality: A Metaphysical Essay* (Oxford, 1930).

150. In Bradley's sense, contradictions exist wherever there is a conjunction of things, a relation, abstracted from the whole of feeling. And contradictions are appearances, not reality. They become real by being included in a whole of feeling, which is both below and above the distinctions of discursive thought, the beginning and the end (see, e.g., *Appearance and Reality*, pp. 500-511).

151. *Appearance and Reality*, pp. 134-36; *Essays*, pp. 10-18.

152. The difference is this: for Bradley, feeling is at the bottom of experience; for scholasticism, mind or intellect is the root of being. Scholasticism takes the principles of reasoning as laws of reality as well as of the mind. It tends to place the whole value of conscious life in the act of knowing. It draws a distinction in kind between sense and perception and intellectual knowledge; and it holds the latter to be superior to the former because the objects it deals with, although abstracted from the world of sense and representing a knowledge of that world, are yet independent of time and space. Further, it is the abstractive nature of the intellect which establishes in reason the spirituality of the soul. See De Wulf, *Philosophy and Civilization in the Middle Ages* (New York, Dovern Publications, Inc., 1953), chap. viii.

153. *Essays*, pp. 219-23, 235.

154. *Ethical Studies* (2nd ed.; Oxford, 1927, reprinted 1935), pp. 219-24; *Essays*, pp. 86-92.

155. *Ethical Studies*, pp. 94-97, 115, 163-65; *The Principles of Logic*, I, 187.

156.. *The Principles of Logic*, I, 340-43.

157. *Ethical Studies*, p. 314. The necessity is both psychological and logical. There is the basic unrest of life, or, what is the same thing, the sense of its contradictions; and there is the setting up of contradiction and coherence as absolute intellectual criteria of truth and reality.

158. *Ethical Studies*, pp. 319, 320. See also pp. 314-20.

159. Eliot: "We may raise the question whether 'literature' exists; but for certain purposes, such as the purpose of this essay on Dante, we must assume that there is literature and literary appreciation; we must assume that the reader can obtain the full 'literary' or (if you will) 'aesthetic' enjoyment without sharing the beliefs of the author. If there is 'literature,' if there is 'poetry,' then it must be possible to have full literary or poetic appreciation without sharing the beliefs of the poet. That is as far as my thesis goes in the present essay. It may be argued whether there is literature, whether there is poetry, and whether there is any meaning in the term 'full appreciation.' But I have assumed for this essay that these things exist and that these terms are understood." (*Selected Essays*, pp. 229-30.)

This is the reason there is no progress in art. Beauty being an immaterial reality—an unseen presence divined by the artist and made visible in his art—it cannot be altered. Beauty, unlike automobiles and refrigerators, is not subject to improvement or deterioration. It has no trade-in value. Cf. Eliot: "He [the poet] must be quite aware of the obvious fact that art never improves, but that the material of art is never quite the same." (*Selected Essays*, p. 6.) Cf. Kant, note 79. Cf. the "Statement by Picasso: 1923," in *Picasso: Fifty Years of His Art*, Alfred H. Barr, Jr. (New York: The Museum of Modern Art), 270-71.

160. *Ethical Studies*, p. 321.

161. *Essays*, p. 88.

162. *Ethical Studies*, p. 326.

163. *Ibid.*, p. 321.

164. *Loc. cit.*

165. *Appearance and Reality*, pp. 140-42.

166. *Ibid.*, pp. 405, 410-12.

167. *Essays*, p. 312.

168. *Appearance and Reality*, p. 411.

169. *Essays*, pp. 312-14; *Appearance and Reality*, pp. 461-62.

170. *Appearance and Reality*, p. 411.

171. *Ibid.*, p. 412.

172. *Ibid.*, pp. 143-44; *The Principles of Logic*, I, 2-8, 67.

173. *Appearance and Reality*, fn., p. 389.

174. *Ibid.*, p. 391.

175. *Ibid.*, pp. 391, 394.

176. *Ibid.*, p. 392.

177. *Essays*, pp. 430-32; *Ethical Studies*, pp. 336-42; *Appearance and Reality*, pp. 399-401.

178. *Essays*, pp. 432-33.

179. *Appearance and Reality*, p. 472; *Essays*, pp. 436-39.

180. p. 314.

181. *Ethical Studies*, p. 340.

182. *Appearance and Reality*, p. 398.

183. *Ethical Studies*, pp. 193, 314.

184. *Appearance and Reality*, pp. 391, 401-2; *Essays*, p. 433.

185. *Essays*, p. 428.

186. *Appearance and Reality*, p. 402.

187. *Ibid.*, pp. 398-99.

188. *Ibid.*, pp. 399-401.

189. *Essays*, pp. 437-38.

190. *Ethical Studies*, p. 322.

191. *Selected Essays*, pp. 321-22.

192. p. 68.

193. *Selected Essays*, p. 230.

194. *Essays*, pp. 3, 4.

195. *Selected Essays*, pp. 363, 366-67.

196. *Essays*, pp. 434-35.

197. *Selected Essays*, pp. 365-66.

198. *Essays*, pp. 3, 438.

199. *The Monist* (October, 1916), Vol. XXVI, No. 4, pp. 534-56, 566-76.

200. *Selected Essays*, pp. 368, 299, 252.

201. *Philosophy and Civilization in the Middle Ages*, p. 198.

202. *The Spirit of Mediaeval Philosophy* (New York: Charles Scribner's Sons, 1936), p. 184.

203. De Wulf, *Philosophy and Civilization in the Middle Ages*, p. 198.

204. See "The Development of Leibniz's Monadism."

205. Gilson, p. 200.

206. Gilson, p. 201.

207. Gilson, p. 202.

208. De Wulf, *Philosophy and Civilization in the Middle Ages,* pp. 229-40.

209. *Ibid.,* p. 215.

210. *Essays,* p. 445.

211. *The Listener,* March 16, 1932, p. 383.

212. *Essays,* pp. 446-47.

213. *Essays,* p. 20.

214. *The Enemy,* I (January, 1927), 16.

215. *Ibid.,* pp. 16-17.

216. *Essays,* p. 19.

217. "The Development of Leibniz's Monadism."

218. *Appearance and Reality,* p. 68.

219. *Selected Essays,* p. 305.

220. *Appearance and Reality,* p. 325.

221. *Ibid.,* p. 400.

222. *Selected Essays,* pp. 317, 323.

223. *Essays,* pp. 312-13.

224. *The Sacred Wood,* p. 125.

Here is one more instance. The similarity in tone is very close, and there is a borrowing of key words. Bradley: "That a man should treat of God and religion in order merely to understand them, and apart from the influence of some other consideration and inducement, is to many of us in part unintelligible, and in part also shocking." "And the idea that Absolutism, as I understand it, can fully warrant relative and inconsistent truths, will to many seem even monstrous." And Eliot: "I dare say that some readers will draw political inferences from this discussion: . . . . The writer himself is not without political convictions and prejudices; but the imposition of them is no part of his present intention. What I try to say is this: here are what I believe to be essential conditions for the growth and for the survival of culture. If they conflict with any passionate faith of the reader—if, for instance, he finds it shocking that culture and equalitarianism should conflict, if it seems monstrous to him that anyone should have 'advantages of birth'—I do not ask him to change his faith, I merely ask him to stop paying lip-service to culture." *(Notes towards the Definition of Culture* [New York: Harcourt, Brace and Co., 1949], pp. 14-15.)

225. *Appearance and Reality,* p. 5.

226. With Bradley, the self, like everything else except the Absolute, is full of contradictions, and hence it is not a self-contained individuality—it is something less than the Absolute. Bradley examines a number of commonly held notions about the self in order to show that there is nothing we can point to as the "essence" of the self which is not implicated in change and alteration. He denies the possibility of any such being as a monad—a "supposed simple being," its unity existing as a unit, and "in some sphere presumably secure from chance and change." Moreover, if there were such a being, it would not solve the questions of "diversity and sameness" which arise in connection with the self.

Bradley employs three distinct notions: finite center, soul, and self. A finite center, though not a soul or self, is the basis of these last. It is a feeling center or felt whole not in time and non-relational. A soul, on the other hand, is a finite center regarded as an object existing in time with an identity of before and after. "And further the soul is a thing distinct from the experiences which it has, which experiences we take not as itself but as its states." A self is different from both finite center and soul. "We have a self whenever within a finite centre there is an object. An object involves opposition, theoretical and practical, and this opposition is to a self, and it must so be felt." A self may endure for only a moment, nor need it imply a memory. "The soul is a self so far as within that soul we have the felt opposition of not-self to self." "The self is a content which falls within the soul, and must, I suppose, in a sense be regarded as its 'state'. Hence, if we forget to distinguish the self from the finite centre, which finite centre, as prolonged, we have turned into the soul-thing, the result is certain disaster." (*Appearance and Reality*, chap. ix; *Essays*, pp. 414-21.)

According to De Wulf, the fundamental doctrine of scholastic metaphysics is that *"the individual alone exists."* "Thus, scholasticism is a pluralistic philosophy, and the sworn enemy of monism, which teaches the fusion of all realities in one." "We are impenetrable and incommunicable substances, or personalities." "The human soul is of a *spiritual* nature, ... *immortal*. Accordingly, a human soul, although it constitutes a whole with the body, is not the result of the chemical, physical, and biological activities which explain organic generation. Aristotle had said that the intellect came from without (θύραθεν). Thomas adds: the soul is created by God." (*Philosophy and Civilization in the Middle Ages*, pp. 195, 210, 211-12.)

227. "That was the Greek way of relieving the hardness and unspirituality of pure form. But it involved to a certain degree the sacrifice of what we call *expression;* and a system of abstraction which aimed always

at the broad and general type, at the purging away from the individual of what belonged only to him, and of the mere accidents of a particular time and place, imposed upon the range of effects open to the Greek sculptor limits somewhat narrowly defined. When Michelangelo came, therefore, with a genius spiritualized by the reverie of the middle age, penetrated by its spirit of inwardness and introspection, living not a mere outward life like the Greek, but a life full of intimate experiences, sorrows, consolations, a system which sacrificed so much of what was inward and unseen could not satisfy him. To him, . . . work which did not bring what was inward to the surface, which was not concerned with individual expression, with individual character and feeling, the special history of the special soul, was not worth doing at all."

"I said that the art of Lucca della Robbia possessed in an unusual measure that special characteristic which belongs to all the workmen of his school, ... They bear the impress of a personal quality, a profound expressiveness, what the French call *intimité*, by which is meant some subtler sense of originality—the seal on a man's work of what is most inward and peculiar in his moods, and manner of apprehension: it is what we call *expression*, carried to its highest intensity of degree. That characteristic is rare in poetry, rarer still in art, rarest of all in the abstract art of sculpture; yet essentially, perhaps, it is the quality which alone makes work in the imaginative order really worth having at all." ("Lucca Della Robbia," *The Renaissance: Studies in Art and Poetry* [London: Macmillan & Co., 1919], pp. 66-67, 71-72.)

228. De Wulf observes that the Western civilization of the thirteenth century "is above all the product of French influence." The masters of scholastic philosophy "were all *educated* in France." The part played by the Germans is negligible. The philosophy the Germans developed is not scholastic philosophy; its source is in the neo-Platonism of the thirteenth century, and it is marked by a leaning toward pantheism as, for instance, in Meister Eckhart (*Op. cit.*, p. 281 f.).

Perhaps this has something to do with Eliot's preference for French rather than German writers, especially French writers with a Catholic bias.

229. *On Poetry and Poets*, p. 245.

230. *Selected Essays*, p. 5.

231. *Loc. cit.* Eliot: "It is a judgment, a comparison, in which two things are measured by each other." Bradley: "We begin with A and B, and we compare them to find the relation between them. But the centre of this synthesis must be a felt basis of quality common to both, and this common basis was implicit in our starting-point. You may indeed determine to compare two terms before you know the special points in which they are comparable; but you cannot perform the actual comparison, until the

terms have been unconsciously apprehended under one aspect. Thus reality appears, not simply as two terms, but as possessing an attribute or group of attributes, which is given with two separate sets of qualities. And in the result this basis through its own activity becomes explicit." (*The Principles of Logic*, II, 493.)

232. See chap. xiv, "What is the Real Julius Caesar?" in *Essays*, pp. 409-27; chap. xviii, "Temporal and Spatial Appearance," in *Appearance and Reality*, pp. 181-96.

Bradley's notion of time, like virtually everything else in his philosophy, derives from his view of immediate experience as non-relational. Speaking of this view, he says: "The doctrine in question, Prof. James stated very candidly, has been advocated by myself since 1883. He seems even to give me the credit of having broken away here from the tradition of my school, and of having, conjointly with M. Bergson though at perhaps an earlier date, originated in modern times the true view ignored by and fatal to idealistic Monism. Now for myself (I am of course not concerned with M. Bergson's attitude) I at once, in the same journal, disclaimed, and I now again emphatically disclaim any such originality. When it was that the view in question was first advocated in modern philosophy, I cannot, I regret to say, inform the reader. But that I myself derived it from Hegel is perfectly certain. If I had ever been asked if it was Hegel's teaching, I should have replied that so much at least was indubitable. . . . The fact, I presume, is this, that Prof. James, like his public, failed to realize the wealth, the variety and the radical differences, which are to be found in that outburst of German philosophy which came after Kant." (*Essays, pp.* 152-53.)

233. Eliot: "Some one has said: 'The dead writers are remote from us because we *know* so much more than they did.' Precisely, and they are that which we know." (*Selected Essays*, p. 6.) Bradley: "At any given period to know more than he did, man must have been more than he was; for a human being is nothing if he is not the son of his time; and he must realize himself as that, or he will not do it at all." (*Ethical Studies*, p. 190.)

234. *A Pluralistic Universe* (New York: Longmans, Green, & Co., 1909), p. 185.

235. *The Principles of Psychology* (2 vols.; New York: Dover Publications, Inc., 1950), I, 158.

236. *Ibid*, I, 161.

237. *A Pluralistic Universe*, pp. 187-88.

238. *The Principles of Psychology*, I, 181, 160, 182.

239. *A Pluralistic Universe*, pp. 208-21, 225-72.

240. "And in what manner can your intuition satisfy the claims of understanding? This, to my mind, forms a wholly insuperable obstacle . . . . And the attempt to find in self-consciousness an apprehension at a level, not below, but above relations—a way of apprehension superior to discursive thought, and including its mere process in a higher harmony—appears to me not successful . . . . Even if your intuition is a fact, it is not an *understanding* of the self or of the world. It is a mere experience, and it furnishes no consistent view about itself or about reality in general." (*Appearance and Reality*, pp. 93-94.)

241. Th. Ribot, *Essay on the Creative Imagination*, trans. Albert H. N. Baron (Chicago: The Open Court Publishing Company, 1906). See Ribot's discussion on complex mental states and chemical combination, chap. v, "The Principle of Unity." Though taking note of James's criticism of the mind as mental chemistry, he thinks the notion is valid (p. 82). For some scholastic comments on chemical change, see De Wulf, *Philosophy and Civilization in the Middle Ages*, pp. 201-7. Bradley considers "chemical union" to be different from association. He thinks that such a union of ideas is improbable, but that it seems to take place with emotions, though even here what occurs may not be a union (*The Principles of Logic*, I, 343-45).

242. *The Principles of Logic*, I, 299-309, 330.

243. *Ibid.*, II, 476-86.

"For Aristotle," Eliot says, "reality is here and now; and the true nature of mind is found in the activity which it exercises. Attempt to analyze the mind, as a thing, and it is nothing. It is an operation. Aristotle's psychology therefore starts with psycho-physics, and ascends to speculative reason. It is only then that we perceive what mind is, and in retrospect find that it was present in the simplest sensation." ("The Development of Leibniz's Monadism.") Whether or not this is Aristotle's view of the mind I am unable to say. It seems to be an instance of Eliot's reading Aristotle in terms of Bradley.

"One aim of this book [*The Principles of Logic*]," says Bradley, "was . . . to show that a truer logic must imply a diverse view [from association] of psychical fact. Judgment and Inference in other words, when interpreted rightly by logic must show their essential nature even at their psychical beginning. They must in an undeveloped form be actually there, and must be really effective at the earliest stage of mental life. This is the conclusion at which the psychological enquiries of this volume are aimed and which they endeavor throughout to enforce."

Bradley goes on to say that, though he never pretended to be an Hegelian, it was in Hegel's psychology that he found the suggestion for his doctrine of the mind—his logic. "To learn that Association holds only between universals was to pass from darkness into light. And Hegel's doctrine of Feeling, as a vague *continuum* below relations, seemed and seems to me to have an importance which really is vital . . . . My knowledge of the history of modern psychology does not, I regret, enable me to say how far here Hegel has followed others, as, I presume, he has followed Aristotle." (*The Principles of Logic,* II, 515.)

244. *Appearance and Reality,* pp. 86-87, 201-2, 208-12; *Essays,* pp. 328-31, 341-42, 350; *The Principles of Logic,* II, 598, 614-17, 666.

245. *Selected Essays,* p. 231.

246. *Ibid.,* p. 8.

247. *Essays,* pp. 167-69.

248. *The Principles of Logic,* II, 443. See also pp. 306-10, 440-46, 476-84.

249. *The Use of Poetry,* pp. 126, 30.

250. *Essays,* p. 168.

251. *Selected Essays,* p. 8.

252. *The Use of Poetry,* pp. 122-23.

253. *Ethical Studies,* p. 244.

254. *Selected Essays,* p. 212.

255. *On Poetry and Poets,* pp. 237-38.

256. *Selected Essays,* p. 269.

257. *Ibid.,* p. 259.

258. *Ibid.,* pp. 208-9.

259. *Ibid.* p. 8.

260. *Ibid.,* p. 209.

Perhaps by "pure imagination" Eliot means imagination, distinct from emotion and desire, presenting objective images. See *The Principles of Logic,* II, 444-45.

261. *Selected Essays,* pp. 298-99.

Eliot reads Donne's poetry in the light of a poetic theory derived from Bradley, but he criticizes Donne the personality in the light of the church and tradition.

262. *Selected Essays,* pp. 262, 263, 256.

263. *Ibid.* p. 267.

264. *Ibid.,* p. 10.

265. *The Use of Poetry,* p. 78.

266. *Ibid.,* pp. 118-19.

267. *The Use of Poetry,* p. 75.

268. *On Poetry and Poets*, p. 93.

269. *Notes towards the Definition of Culture*, p. 68.

270. *Essays*, 171-78, 192-98.

271. *Ibid.*, pp. 30-35, 46-48; *Selected Essays*, p. 10.

"At bottom," Bradley says, "the Real is what we feel, and there is no reality outside of feeling. And in the end the Reality (whatever else we say of it) is experience." "It is reality and myself in unbroken unity. We in a sense transcend this unity; . . . . But that we should ever in any way reach a reality outside of it, seems impossible." "Above relations and inclusive of them, there is an Experience which reasserts our original unity."

"But on the other hand the religious consciousness is a whole which includes and is superior to the opposition of its subordinate elements. The terror of sin, for instance, and the wrath of God belong inseparably to one substantial unity, and this unity further can be experienced, can be known and felt in some measure as overriding each aspect . . . . Further, . . . to assume certainty and reality in the case at any rate of my personality seems quite untenable. To identify myself with my feeling centre would be, for example, to fall into ruinous error. For within that centre is experienced the real presence of the whole Universe, including God and my self; and, further, that self is but a limited construction, more or less ill-defined and precarious, built one-sidedly out of materials which fall within my centre." "And the independent reality of the individual . . . is in truth mere illusion." (*Essays*, pp. 315-16, 434.)

God and the Absolute, with Bradley, are the objects respectively of the religious and the philosophic consciousness. Again, neither feeling nor intuition is a medium of revelation about the self or the world; the criterion of truth—the ideal aspect of Reality—is theory.

272. *The Use of Poetry*, p. 27.

273. Bradley, in the course of explaining that reasoning involves, besides analysis and synthesis, a third principle—"the leap of transition from the possible to the real"—says of synthesis taken by itself: "For the whole, which you have reached, is no system of differences; it is not an individual. The differences are an aggregate, found conjoined together, and no self-analysis of a single unity. The elements certainly are united by a central point, and are thus interrelated; but their relations remain external and forced. Instead of moving freely from one to the rest, you are compelled to pass through a machinery of steps, which seem to have no vital connection with the elements you bring together. Thus the union is in the end no inward bond, but a foreign coupling; and you can not pass from the centre to the system of differences. It is

no living point that withdraws into itself the life of its members, and flows forth into a body which it feels as its own. It is the axle of a wheel where spokes are driven in, and where the number of holes and spokes is indifferent." *(The Principles of Logic,* II, 488.)

274. *The Use of Poetry,* pp. 144-45.

275. For a useful comment on Eliot's poetry see I. A. Richards, *Principles of Literary Criticism* (New York: Harcourt, Brace & Co., 1947), pp. 289-95.

276. "The Music of Poetry," *On Poetry and Poets;* "The Modern Mind" and "Conclusion," *The Use of Poetry.*

277. *Selected Essays,* pp. 352-57; *The Use of Poetry,* p. 26.

278. *On Poetry and Poets,* p. 250.

279. Eliot prefers Wordsworth to Coleridge. He is not unappreciative of Coleridge's genius; and the interest Coleridge as a critic holds for him has continued to grow. But he prefers Wordsworth because Wordsworth is the more traditional poet and critic. In his opinion, what gives Wordsworth the "highest place" as a critic is not his social interests, which account for his views on poetic diction and choice of poetic subjects, but the "profound spiritual revival" present in the Preface and his poetry. This seems to be an expression of Eliot's bias for what is European as against the non-scholastic German tradition. It is evinced in his attitude toward Goethe and toward the German idealism in Coleridge's theory of fancy and imagination. Coleridge's theory of fancy and imagination, in Eliot's view, on one side is infected by empirical psychology and on the other by German idealism. Wordsworth succeeded in working his way out of pantheism.

280. *After Strange Gods,* pp. 18-20, 31, 36.

281. *Selected Essays,* pp. 31-32.

282. *The Use of Poetry,* p. 84. "The Metaphysical Poets," *Selected Essays;* "Milton I" and "Milton II," *On Poetry and Poets.*

283. *Selected Essays,* pp. 134, 136, 137.

284. *Ibid.,* p. 118.

285. "Religion and Literature," *op. cit.,* pp. 347, 348.

286. *Ibid.,* p. 343.

287. *Selected Essays,* pp. 117-18.

288. *Ibid.,* p. 108.

289. *Ibid.,* p. 402.

290. J. E. Spingarn, *A History of Literary Criticism in the Renaissance,* (2nd ed., New York: Columbia University Press, 1949), p. 312.

291. Edward K. Rand, "The Classics in European Education," in *The Greek Genius and its Influence: Selected Essays and Extracts,* ed. Lane Cooper (New Haven: Yale University Press, 1928), pp. 189-90.

INDEX

Absolute, the, 84, 94, 95, 98, 105, 106, 111, 115, 118, 136, 141, 164, 209, 215, 220

Absolutism, 108, 115, 214

Action, the quality of, in tragedy and comedy, 19, 21

Addison, 142

Aesthetic: attitude, 95-96; enjoyment, 212; fact, 196; interest, 208; object, 98; pleasure, 174, 177; point of view, 79, 176, 177, 181, 203; sensibility, 205; state, 97; theories, 80

Aesthetics, 79, 94, 142, 146, 147, 170, 182, 210; as a branch of psychology, 143; defined, by Baumgarten, 25; general, 7, 77; of Italy, 207; the limits of, 86; and logic, 25, 26, 29, 30, 31, 32, 33, 41, 63, 201; a mixed study, 80; modern philosophic, 24; as philosophy, differentiated from literary criticism and the history of literature, 7, 190. *See also* 27-76

Agamemnon, 150

Agamemnon, 150

Aistheta, 27, 193

American pragmatism, 89. *See also* pragmatists.

Andrewes, Lancelot, 117, 159

Anglican church, 109

Anti-intellectualism, 145

Anti-positivists, 145

Aquinas, St. Thomas, 115, 122, 209, 215

Aristophanes, 20

		DATE DUE	